AMERICA'S REPUBLICAN FORM OF GOVERNMENT

KURT ST. ANGELO

America's Republican Form of Government

Library of Congress Cataloging in Publication Data
St. Angelo, Kurt, 1955 - [1]
     America's Republican Form of Government – Kurt St.
        Angelo
     Includes bibliographical references and index
     ISBN-13: 978-1539786368, ISBN-10: 1539786366
          1. Law, republican form of government, 2. Law,
          natural and positive law, 3. Law, constitu-
          tional law

ISBN-13: 978-1539786368
ISBN-10: 1539786366
Library of Congress Control Number: 2016918411

TABLE OF CONTENTS

Introduction

This book is about the government to which Americans pledge their support in the *Pledge of Allegiance.* [2] It is about the criteria for new states in the Northwest Ordinance of 1787, which required that "the constitution and government so to be formed, shall be republican..." It is about the Guaranty Clause at Article IV, Section 4 of the U.S. Constitution that requires Congress to "guarantee to every State of the Union a Republican Form of Government..."

This book defines that republican form.

Logically, the above important references to the republican form of government allude to something specific, with a definite meaning. Logically, the republican form is not a political question, which is subject to a legislature's definition, or its meaning would be changeable and indefinite.

Consistent with this logic, *Bouvier's Law Dictionary* states that the guarantee of a republican form of government "supposes a form already established..." [3] This suggests that the republican form is not defined by the legislative branch, but is an inherent constitutionally-established form that is to be discerned and secured by the judicial branch.

This is also the view of the U.S. Supreme Court in *Minor v. Happersett* (1875). Although this case incorrectly denied female *natural born Citizen* Virginia Minor the right to vote, the Court nonetheless contended that the term *republican* has an inherent meaning. In denying Minor the right to vote based on history, the Court wrote that "it is certainly now too late to contend that a government is not republican, within the meaning of this guaranty in the constitution, because women are not made voters." [4]

In other words, wrote the *Minor* Court, the Guaranty Clause of the U.S. Constitution supposes a fixed definition of the republican form of government. However, the Court did not attempt to define this form, and therefore overlooked an inher-

5

ent feature of all republics, i.e., natural political equality.

This is the idea that male and female natural born Citizens have the same political rights in a republic, and that female natural born Citizens, who inherit their political rights from their citizen parents, naturally inherit these rights equally with their male siblings. Natural republican citizens - as opposed to naturalized, artificial citizens - naturally inherit their political rights, just as they do their fingers and toes, which rights are naturally the same for all such citizens.

Consistent with the *Minor* decision, this book stands for the idea that the republican form of government can be judicially discerned, and that the enforcement of the Guaranty Clause is not a political question at all. In fact, the republican form exists only when legislatures are excluded from legislating over certain subject matter, such as citizens' constitutional rights.

And if the premises of *Bouvier's Law Dictionary* and of the *Minor* Court are correct, i.e., that reference to a republican form of government in the U.S. Constitution "supposes a form already established...," [5] then likewise, the U.S. Constitution supposes that the meanings of other words and terms in it – such as *case, controversy, criminal case, crime, offense, property, regulate, prohibit,* and *natural born Citizens* – are also already established, and are also not subject to Congress as political questions. For example, the Supreme Court wrote in *U.S. v. Wong Kim Ark* (1898) that natural born Citizenship is determined "under the circumstances defined in the constitution," [6] and not by Congress.

Likewise the republican form and the other above constitutional terms do not exist to be defined by Congress or state legislatures. In fact, none of their meanings are political questions that are subject to definition by the legislative branch of America's fifty-one republican governments. To the contrary, Congress and all American government officials exist to know and enforce the natural meaning of these terms – so as to guarantee the republican form of government to U.S. citizens.

My path to discerning the republican form of government has been long and winding. As a law student, and even as a Government major in college, the topic was never vetted.

Even after reading and discussing Plato's *Republic* during college, I was left with the questions: What is a republic, and what makes one so special? This book answers both questions.

I came to understand the meaning of America's special republican form of government about three years ago, while writing my previous book *BUSTED – A Whistleblower's Guide to the War on Drugs.* [7] In that book I show that America's drug war exists only because government officials do not follow the Controlled Substances Act and other drug statutes.

Far from criminalizing drugs within America's states, these republican statutes secure 1) drug users' constitutional right to acquire, possess and use drugs, and 2) unwanted drug dealers' 14th Amendment equal right to administrative due process, just like pharmaceutical companies receive.

America's false enforcement of drug statutes occurs because American attorneys do not know how America's republics are to operate, which matter is particularly relevant to criminal law. Nor do they understand Congress' relationship to the states, called federalism. Unaware of the various separations of power that ensure America's republican form of government, most have literally been unable to properly read and understand U.S. and state drug statutes, which carry out or fulfill this form.

The primary and most important separation of power that is discernible in republican law, including in America's drug statutes, is that between legislators' positive (written) law authority and individuals' natural law authority. This will be thoroughly explained. Without knowledge and recognition of this natural law jurisdiction, then attorneys have been incapable of administering the republican form of government, which is a birthright of America's natural law citizens.

Realizing that there is not only a positive law (legislative) jurisdiction within the U.S. and state constitutions, but also a natural law jurisdiction, was central to my understanding of the republican form. This natural law jurisdiction first came to me by reading the natural born Citizen Clause at Article II, Section 1 of the U.S. Constitution.

This clause shows that there are two kinds of U.S. citizens, each from a different source. There are citizens who inherit their political rights under natural law (called *natural born Citizens*) and there are adopted citizens who are granted their rights by U.S. positive law (called *Citizens of the United States*). Thus, there are two jurisdictions – natural law and positive law – that define republican citizens.

The political rights of all U.S. citizens are defined by one or the other of these jurisdictions. In a republic, in addition to defining natural born Citizens, natural law also defines such concepts as crime, property, production and marriage.

Knowing this is essential to understanding and upholding the republican form of government. Without knowledge of the separation of positive and natural law, as well as many other separations of power embodied in America's constitutions, then American attorneys do not – because they cannot – administer republican justice. Because they do not properly conceive it, then they have not been able to properly secure it, which in fact is their sworn duty.

Because the republican form of government is the only sane and moral form of government, then every country on Earth should adopt it. Because this book is likely the first to detail the republican form, then it is a book for the whole world.

I take no personal credit for the information in this book, or the ability to write it. With the help of Jesus of Nazareth, Richard Hooker, William Blackstone, John Locke, Thomas Jefferson, and certainly my parents, I merely discerned most of the characteristics of the republican form and wrote them down.

So, while this book offers some very unique and important information, it is not the product of my original thinking. Like the republican form itself, most of it supposes a wise pre-

8

exising form of thinking that had already been established, only to be rediscovered.

This book is to discover what at least some of the Founding Fathers of the United States had in mind when they agreed upon the U.S. Constitution. This book is also to reprise their knowledge of government. Explaining their masterpiece fulfills my life as a student of Government and Law.

My role in these pages is analogous to removing layers of whitewash that cover a magnificent mural. As I scratch, peel and dissolve away the layers of past neglect, ignorance and faulty logic, the rich colors and texture of the republican form of government show through. I promise that properly understanding this governmental form will improve readers' views of both American law and their own political worth.

Two kinds of law

To know the republican form of government is to know *law*. The U.S. Supreme Court has called law the definition and limitation of power. [8] Law is about power and duty to power.

The first rule of law is that there is only one sovereign power over any particular subject matter or territory. Each duty that one owes is owed to only one sovereign.

A sovereign is defined as a person, body or state in which supreme or ultimate authority is vested. [9] It is the who or the what that has plenary authority to legislate (create) or adjudicate (judge) any particular subject matter. Plenary means "full, entire, complete, absolute, perfect, unqualified." [10]

Given these definitions of law and sovereignty, there are basically two sovereigns in this world: nature and Man. And there are two kinds of law: natural (unwritten) law and Man's positive (written) law.

Natural law is nature's inherent power that operates without having to be written down. It manifests as the physical, cognitive, emotional and political laws of nature. [11]

9

Natural law applies to natural things and persons. In the United States, it defines all of natural persons' natural political rights and their duties to other people. Such rights include their natural freedoms (called natural rights); their substantive rights that are secured in state constitutions, in the Bill of Rights (Amendments 1 – 10 to the U.S. Constitution), and in the 13th Amendment; and their rights of political participation such as the rights to vote and run for President.

(These are political rights because they exist in a polity. Rights and duties are political when they relate to other people.)

In contrast, positive law is enacted written law that applies to the government and to artificial persons that are created by positive law. *Black's Law Dictionary* defines artificial persons as "persons created and devised by human laws for the purposes of society and government, as distinguished from natural persons." [12] Positive law for government and for artificial persons manifests in constitutions, statutes and regulations.

In the United States such artificial persons include 1) all commercial enterprises, such as partnerships, corporations and limited liability companies, and 2) all persons who require governments' permission to exist or operate within the United States. This latter group includes all foreigners (also called aliens), all licensed professionals, all permit holders, all income taxpayers, and all licensed automobile drivers, to name a few.

These artificial persons have all consented to the jurisdiction over commerce or immigration of American legislatures, which power has been constitutionally granted by U.S. citizens. We know all such artificial persons by the numbers that have been assigned to them. Natural persons can be counted under law, for example for a capitation tax, but they are not naturally numbered. Being numbered is an attribute of positive law only.

Positive law (and its artificial definitions and numbering systems) do not apply to natural persons. Instead, positive law defines artificial persons and their artificial rights and duties. Thus positive legislative law does not define natural persons' natural rights and duties, which need not be written down.

Because law imposes duty, then there are two kinds of duties: 1) natural law duties and 2) artificial, positive law duties. The former are natural duties that we owe to others. The latter are legal or equitable duties owed to artificial persons.

Natural law duties are not legal duties. Each kind of duty comes from a different source. Natural law duties are imposed by nature, while artificial, legal duties are imposed by Man.

As we shall see, the words law and legal operate in separate judicial jurisdictions. The word law applies to natural persons and to natural law, while the word legal applies to artificial persons and to positive law. What is legal for artificial persons is different than what is lawful for natural persons, who are also referred to as individuals.

Individuals owe natural duties. For example, we all have a natural duty to eat food and drink water. We must fulfill these duties, or we die. As well, men have a natural political duty to defend territory that they have staked out, or they and their families may die.

Likewise, parents have a natural duty to care for their children. Conversely, it is not women's natural duty to defend a man-made border, or for non-parents to care for other people's children, although they may choose to.

Lex spectat natura ordinem, says a legal maxim. *The law regards the order of nature.* This natural order and the duties that it imposes not need to be written down to operate.

The Creator "has laid down only such laws as were founded in those relations of justice, that existed in the nature of things antecedent to any positive precept," wrote Sir William Blackstone in his *Commentaries on the Laws of England* (1752).[13]

In fact, before kings such as Hammurabi (c. 1810 – 1750 BCE) and prophets such as Moses (c. 1201 BCE), these duties were not written down. Parents naturally raised their own children and men defended their society's boundaries – all without positive law telling them to.

So natural rights and duties come naturally. They pre-date all of Man's positive law, and thus are not creations of positive law. Political leaders may write down these natural rights and duties for people to read and observe, but such leaders did not and do not create (invent, legislate) them.

This means that a legislature's writing down of such natural duties does not constitute positive law, but amounts merely to the codification of natural law. For example, murder was naturally prohibited in Babylon and Egypt long before it was first written (or etched) into the Hammurabi Code and into the Ten Commandments.

Hammurabi and Moses merely wrote down or codified what was already a natural duty to not murder. (As a king, Hammurabi also threw some unnatural, artificial duties into his code.) Likewise, America's criminal statutes merely codify what is already naturally wrong, which is to injure others.

In contrast, only artificial persons owe artificial, legal duties. Artificial persons, such as corporations, licensed professionals and licensed motor vehicle drivers, are creations of positive law. That is why they are regulated.

Positive law is 1) that which is written down by a political sovereign or its agents, such as legislatures and regulators, and 2) that which imposes or creates artificial, legal rights and duties in artificial persons. For example, the requirement to drive below posted speed limits is a legal duty that is imposed upon licensed drivers, which duty does not apply to their un-licensed passengers or to people walking their dogs.

Thus, positive law does not apply to natural persons when acting in their natural capacities, such as sitting as a passenger in a car or walking to a store. Nor does it impose either natural duties upon natural persons, such as the duty to sleep, or artificial duties upon natural persons, such as the duty to wear a seat belt in a car or to use a cane while walking.

All artificial, legal duties are imposed upon artificial persons acting in artificial capacities, such as licensed drivers when operating registered motor vehicles. Those persons are legally responsible for posted speed limits, for legislated duties to not text-while-driving, for wearing eyeglasses if required, and for their passengers' use of seat belts, for instance.

The latter, who are acting in their natural capacities, do not owe positive law duties to the positive law sovereign, which does not license or regulate their sitting. While sitting in a passenger seat, they are not directly subject to positive law and to being ticketed. In an American republic, they are only beholden to the natural law of the natural sovereign, which tells them when to request a food- or restroom-stop.

Nature imposes certain natural duties on all of us. In a republic, it does not impose artificial duties upon natural persons, such as 1) the duty to file forms, 2) the duty to register with a government agency, 3) the duty to seek government's permission to purchase any kind of personal property, or 4) the duty to purchase such property from particular people.

These are examples of subject matter within individuals' natural personal jurisdiction – outside of the scope of positive law. In a republic, it is imperative for Man's positive law to recognize these natural separations of power.

Because law is the definition of power, then natural law is the power that can be naturally discerned through observation and analysis of nature. Such observation and analysis define this natural power, called the laws of nature.

The laws of nature include 1) nature's physical laws, such as gravity, thermodynamics and animals' need for water, food and oxygen, 2) nature's cognitive laws, such as logic and reason, 3) nature's emotional laws, such as empathy, revenge and attraction, and 4) nature's political laws, which define our fundamental rights and duties. [14]

America's *Declaration of Independence* (1776) is an expression of nature's political laws. The *Declaration*'s use of the term "the Laws of Nature" as a proper noun refers to the political laws of nature. I will use these terms interchangeably.

Through observation and analysis of nature, the *Declaration* holds that certain truths are self-evident: that all natural persons are created equal and that each of us is endowed by our Creator (or nature) with certain natural, inherent and unalienable rights. It is as Thomas Jefferson wrote that: "A free people [claim] their rights as derived from the laws of nature, and not as the gift from their chief magistrate." [15]

"TO understand political power right, and derive it from its original," wrote John Locke in his *Second Treatise on Civil Government* (1690), "we must consider, what state all men are naturally in, and that is, a state of perfect freedom to order their actions, and dispose of their possessions and persons, as they think fit, within the bounds of the law of nature, without asking leave, or depending upon the will of any other man." [16]

So, wrote Locke, political power derives from the state of nature – the "state all men are naturally in" – where they are free "to order their actions, and dispose of their possessions . . . without asking leave, or depending upon the will of any other man" . . . "within the bounds of the law of nature." [17].

To maintain this natural state of liberty is why the republican form of government was created in the United States. It exists to secure people's natural rights – their rights to order their own actions and dispose of their property – without asking anyone's permission, but within the bounds of the law.

In the state of Indiana – which is my home state and whose law I will generally use here to represent the law of other American state republics – these natural rights include the well known rights to life, liberty and the pursuit of happiness. [18]

They also include the natural right to acquire and possess personal property. The Indiana Constitution (1816) says that people have a natural, unalienable and inherent right to acquire, possess and defend property. [19] Most American state constitutions have references to these same natural rights.

These natural rights are not subject to the positive law of a legislature, as explained by the Indiana Supreme Court in

14

Beebe v. State of Indiana (1855). "There are certain absolute rights," wrote the Court, "and the right of property is among them, which in all free governments, must of necessity be protected from legislative interference, irrespective of constitutional checks and guards." [20]

Beebe shows that natural political law is immutable. As we shall see, Man's positive law has no authority within a republic over the power of nature and its laws, including its natural political laws. That is why republics separate the power of natural law from that of positive law, which is embodied in the separation between the law and equity jurisdictions.

As well, positive law may not violate natural law in any manner. For example, neither a king nor a legislature can decree gravity to not exist, or for hunger to be vanquished, or for 2 plus 2 to equal 5. And as the story goes, emperors who wear no clothes cannot change the reality that they are naked.

Nor can legislatures' positive law violate the political laws of nature. For example, positive law cannot decree rights to be wrongs and wrongs to be rights. Nor can it equate adopted citizens with natural born ones, or positive law rights with natural rights. There are natural, obvious and objective separations between these concepts that we cannot ignore.

Natural law exists to be discerned or discovered. It is not fabricated or decreed. Through observation and analysis, its sciences – including its social sciences – "study the structure and behavior of the physical and natural world..." [21]

As we shall see, many constitutional concepts in the United States are discerned from – and defined by – natural political law, and not by Man's law. For example, natural law defines (in context) each of the following words from American constitutions, e.g., case, controversy, crime, offense, felony, misdemeanor, injury, victim, natural right, slavery, property, and natural born Citizen.

Natural law also defines other law concepts that are not found in most of America's constitutions, such as voluntary, contract, male, female, marriage, nation, production, and alien. These and the above words are natural law terms because they are facts of nature, defined and provable by objective criteria.

Their meanings naturally existed and were agreed upon before American positive law was ever written down. As with the meanings of other natural phenomenon, they are inherent.

Like the concepts of dark and light, these words, their meanings and their use predate all current earthly governments. America's constitutions codify these words' natural meanings to secure justice for natural persons. When American legislatures codify natural law that applies to individuals, then they have no constitutional authority to change the meanings of these words.

In contrast, when legislating positive law that applies to artificial persons, then American legislatures can declare dark to be light. As creations of positive law, all artificial persons within the United States answer to the positive law definitions of American legislatures. Artificial persons are as their legislative sovereigns define them.

Likewise, natural persons are as nature defines them. Individuals answer to natural law definitions. This makes these definitions to be checks upon the positive law authority of Man and the standard for positive law's legitimacy. Republican legislatures cannot decree light to be dark, or mothers to be fathers, or aliens to be natural born when writing down rules for natural persons, who are owed natural justice.

That some things are subject to natural law and other things are subject to positive law was discerned by the prophet Jesus of Nazareth over two thousand years ago. During his life (4 BCE – 30 CE), Rome levied an imperial tax upon non-Romans.

Jesus opposed this artificial duty. He claimed the natural right to worship his God without having to pay a tribute to Rome. He said to "render unto Caesar the things that are Caesar's, and unto God the things that are God's." [22]

This was to say that some things answer to the authority of God (or nature) and other things are subject to Caesar (or

Man's positive law). Understanding law is to first know which sovereign is in charge of what. That there are two sovereigns that create rights and duties in people was a self-evident political truth for Jesus, which he discerned from observation and analysis of his natural political reality.

To sum up this section, there are two kinds of law and two kinds of persons. Natural law applies to natural persons exercising their natural rights in their natural capacities. Positive law applies to artificial persons exercising artificial privileges, called legal or equitable rights, granted from an artificial political sovereign.

Jesus claimed that his worship of God was not a legal right that was granted from Rome, and was thus not subject to its positive law and taxes. That is what the 1st Amendment to the U.S. Constitution in part also says.

Every creation of nature, such as natural persons and natural law citizens, are subject to natural political law. Every creation of positive law, such as corporations or naturalized citizen-subjects, are subject to positive law.

Creations of nature, acting in their natural capacities, are not subject to positive law. Positive law does not include codified natural law. Natural rights and duties are self-evident law, but which are written down for mankind's convenience.

Natural political law

We hold these truths to be self-evident that nature imposes natural law duties upon natural persons. Most obvious among these are the natural duties to eat, drink, excrete, sleep, exercise and breathe. We owe these to nature, or our nature.

These physical duties are mandatory. People are also duty-bound by gravity and other physical forces. They naturally react to hormonal urges and blood-sugar surges. These are just some of mankind's duties to the physical laws of nature.

As law is the definition of power, then these duties in

part define nature's power over mankind. What power is left to individuals is called free will.

Essentially, people's free will is bounded on one side by their duties to nature and on the other side by the duties that they owe to other people by consent, for example by contract. (Free will does not exist under a condition of slavery, domination or coercion.)

So, free will is an individual's power (jurisdiction) in a state of natural liberty between that which is naturally compulsory, such as having to sleep, and that which is owed due to voluntary consent, such as working for someone. One may be free of one's consensual duties, such as getting a vacation from work, but never be free of one's duties to nature.

As scientists over time have tried to discern the physical laws of nature, we can also discern the existence of natural political laws, called the Laws of Nature, through observation and analysis of mankind's political action. We can discern natural political rules by observing behavior that is under the authority of all natural persons, which is their free will.

Through observation of mankind in their free state, several things become self-evident. First, it is apparent that individuals can exercise their free will to the extent that such exercise does not interfere with others' free will. As the saying goes, one's rights end where others' rights begin.

This rule is naturally self-proving because otherwise – that is, under the opposite rule where some people can exercise arbitrary physical power over others and their property – then communities would self-destruct from predatory chaos. So we naturally have a duty to not harm one another and their interests, or living with one another would be intolerable.

Also self-evident is that this right and duty are equal among all humans. Everyone has an equal natural right to exercise free will and an equal natural duty to not violate this same natural right of other people. Because this political rule applies to everyone, then there is self-evident equality under natural political law.

As described by John Locke, this natural state is "of equality, wherein all the power and jurisdiction is reciprocal, no one having more than another; there being nothing more evident, than that creatures of the same species and rank, promiscuously born to all the same advantages of nature, and the use of the same faculties, should also be equal one amongst another without subordination or subjection..." [23]

This is in part to what Thomas Jefferson and the other founders of the United States referred in the *Declaration of Independence*, as it reads: "WE hold these Truths to be self-evident, that all Men are created equal..."

They knew that we must all be equally bound from violating the rights of others, which is a rule of natural law, or society would degenerate into the law of the jungle, which is the rule between predator and prey instead of political equals. It is "that all men may be restrained from invading others' rights, and from doing hurt to one another, and the law of nature be observed, which willeth the peace and preservation of all mankind," wrote Locke. [24]

The highest expression of this natural law duty to respect the rights of others is called the Golden Rule, which is to do unto others as we wish they would do unto us. The Golden Rule is best known in western civilization because the prophet Jesus of Nazareth preached it, and because it is a tenet of Christianity.

However, Jesus did not make up or invent the Golden Rule. Because it is a self-evident political law of nature, Jesus merely discerned it. And because the Golden Rule is attributed to Confucius (551 – 479 BCE), then Jesus did not discern it first.

For purposes of law, the Golden Rule means to do others no harm. It means that all relationships require our voluntary consent, just as each of us would wish to be treated.

Jesus realized that if people could follow just one rule, i.e. to not harm other people, then we would have perfect natural justice. There would be no violence, theft or fraud. Everyone would treat everyone else equally and morally.

Likewise, if everyone practiced not harming others, then there would be little need for a justice system 1) because there would be no crime or uncompensated injury, and 2) because all disagreements could be voluntarily resolved.

No one would be a slave to anyone else, and no one would be forced to do things against their will, due to others' superior power. Such a world would exist by the rule of natural law instead of the law among non-reasoning animals.

Sixteenth century British theologian Richard Hooker described the Golden Rule in this manner: that one's "desire therefore to be loved" imposes upon one "a natural duty of bearing to them-ward fully the like affection." This creates a "relation of equality" such "(t)hat because we would take no harm, we must therefore do none." [25]

Jesus put it more simply in this way: "Love thy enemy as thyself." [26]   At Matthew 22: 35 – 40, a lawyer asked Jesus about the greatest duty ("commandment") in the law, to which Jesus responded:

> "Thou shallt love the Lord thy God with all thy heart, and with all thy soul, and with all thy mind. This is the first and great commandment. And the second is like unto it. Thou shallt love thy neighbor as thyself. On these two commandments hang all the law..."

These are natural commandments. Said Jesus, they come from God. Wrote Jefferson in the *Declaration of Independence,* they come from "nature's God."

On these same two natural commandments hang all republican law. They reflect the role of God's law, i.e. natural law, in an organized society, as well as the need to love oneself and one's fellow Man, at least enough to do them no harm.

Thus, the Golden Rule reflects the highest natural political duty that individuals owe to society and one another. It is a political duty because we live in polities, which is short for organized societies. To do no harm is what politics requires – both naturally and universally – from each of us.

The Golden Rule also reflects the natural equal order because – we must morally assume that – it is not in human nature to wish to be born a slave or to be subject to the will of others. To think otherwise, i.e., to think that certain natural persons should be born subject to others, is to worship the laws of Man instead of the equal *natura ordinem*. [27]

As the Golden Rule is our natural standard for moral behavior, then violations of the Golden Rule are the natural standard for morally bad behavior. In law, behavior which is inherently or naturally wrong is called *malum in se*. (It will later be distinguished from *malum prohibita*.)

To harm other people either negligently or intentionally is *malum in se*. Harming others is the natural standard for civil and criminal wrongness. Natural law determines good from bad, and public right from public wrong.

"These are the eternal, immutable laws of good and evil, to which the Creator Himself in all his dispensations conforms," wrote Blackstone in his *Commentaries*, "and which He has enabled human reason to discover, so far as they are necessary for the conduct of human actions." [28]

For two people to angrily yell at one another is perhaps a violation of the Golden Rule, but American law takes cognizance of that *malum in se* which violates the rights of others, i.e., that which trespasses against their person, reputation or property.

For example, the Indiana Constitution says that the state's judicial courts are open to injury to one's person, property or reputation. [29] This means that they are not open for people merely yelling at one another.

Essentially, Americans have a natural right to do anything natural except for natural wrongs. It is a natural wrong, i.e., *malum in se*, to violate anyone else's natural rights.

21

Physical violations of others' rights are called torts, which are actionable wrongs. The most egregious torts are intentional ones, called crimes.

"In all cases, the crime includes an injury," wrote Blackstone in his *Commentaries*. "Every public offense is also a private wrong, and somewhat more; it affects the individual, and it likewise affects the community." [30]

This is reiterated in *Corpus Juris Secundum*, as quoted by the Indiana Supreme Court.

> "The distinction between torts and crimes is based upon the public nature of the criminal offense. 'Although the same act may constitute both a crime and a tort, the crime is an offense against the public pursued by the sovereign, while the tort is a private injury which is pursued by the injured party.' 14 Am. Jur. 755, § 3. The same distinction has been noted by another authority in the following language: 'Therefore, the real distinction between a tort and a crime is to be sought for, not in a difference between their tendencies, but in the difference between the methods by which the remedy for the wrong is pursued, a wrong for which the remedy is pursued by and at the discretion of the individual injured or his representative being a tort, and a wrong for which the wrongdoer is proceeded against by the sovereign or state for the purpose of punishment being a crime.' 16 C.J. § 3; 22 C.J.S., Criminal Law, § 4." [31]

In other words, wrote the Indiana Supreme Court, there is no "real distinction between a tort and a crime" except between "the public nature of the criminal offense" and "the methods by which the remedy for the wrong is pursued..." [32] Both torts and crimes are injurious "wrongs." [33] All crimes are torts.

American Jurisprudence 2nd reiterates this. It says that a "crime is said to be an offense against the sovereign, a wrong which the government deems injurious not only to the victim but to the public at large..." [34]

The clause "not only to the victim" signifies that all crimes, by definition, injure natural persons or their rights as a condition precedent before the public-at-large is deemed injured. The public has rights only to the extent of the natural duty of all persons to refrain from harming the physical and political rights of others.

Thus, all injurious behavior is naturally prohibited. And all predatory behavior – which is to intentionally use force, theft or fraud to violate others' rights – is naturally criminally prohibited. (Fraud is to intentionally misrepresent the truth of something so as to deprive another of a right.)

One of the roles of republican government is to enforce these natural prohibitions of torts and crimes. Said another way, one of republics' roles is to enforce this prohibition of natural crime, defined by injury.

It is not the role of republican government to make up artificial crimes so as to incarcerate innocent disfavored people, which would be predatory. Thus, this rule of natural law minimizes the law of predator over prey. Wrote Locke, it serves to "preserve the innocent and restrain offenders." [35]

Logic and reason also show us that positive law, which is Man's written law for artificial persons, does not determine right and wrong, good or bad, and what is allowed or prohibited in a republic. What is civilly and criminally prohibited, i.e., injuring others' rights, is naturally prohibited.

American legislatures merely write down these natural prohibitions, give them names and assign them degrees of punishment. They do not create them. Nature does.

This is to reiterate that legislatures are not the source of people's natural rights and duties. They are not the source of our duty to not commit crimes and other torts. Nature is.

People had these natural duties before governments were

created. As Blackstone noted, these duties "existed in the nature of things antecedent to any positive precept." [36]

Harmful behavior is naturally prohibited because it obviously violates natural law's mandate to do no harm. The positive law authority may not legitimately make such harmful behavior lawful because what is lawful and unlawful, or good and *malum in se,* are defined by the political laws of nature.

For example, America's legislatures may not immunize people to commit murder, theft or rape. This is because the power to define crime – and who is a criminal – is not within their legislative authority. Nature defines who is criminal in a republic, not Man. By definition, criminals harm other people.

Crime is defined by natural law, and not by the arbitrary standards of a legislature. It is to violate someone else's natural rights. American legislatures merely write down crimes (and their proportional punishment) so that people need not look up these standards in judicial case law. Crime's natural definition, which always includes injury, determines the subject matter jurisdiction (adjudicatory power) of judicial criminal courts.

Thus, the positive law of legislatures has no effect upon what is right or wrong, or what is allowed or prohibited by Nature and its criminal law. What is morally bad and criminal is determined by a natural standard, and not by Man.

This natural standard to do no harm is discerned from applying logic and reason to the observation of human behavior. It is an eternal, immutable law of good and evil "to which the Creator Himself ... enabled human reason to discover...," wrote Blackstone. [37]

"The like natural inducement hath brought men to know that it is no less their duty, to love others than themselves," wrote Richard Hooker, as quoted by Locke. [38]

Thus, to leave the law of the jungle, which is the law of predator over prey, and to enter the rule of law, which is the rule of natural law based on political equality, requires adopting the Golden Rule as the law standard, just as Jesus said. And as we shall see, this simple natural rule is the essence of both political morality and moral government based on equality.

Under the natural laws of compensation and retaliation, which are better known as "an eye-for-an-eye," yelling at one another warrants only reciprocal yelling. It is physical violations of the Golden Rule and others' natural rights that naturally invoke America's justice systems.

Conversely, to claim that positive law – that is, the law of Man – has any authority to define criminal right and wrong – as well as the jurisdiction of criminal courts – would defy observation. Legislatures can no more deny our natural law duties to one another than to legislate against the laws of physics.

So, it is self-evident that nature has sovereignty over certain subject matter, over which man's deliberative bodies do not. Man's artificial positive law has no authority over our hunger, our sexual biases, our sleep patterns, our proclivity to intoxicate, or what we want to purchase. Nor has it authority to define right and wrong, or what is criminal or not criminal. Ultimately there is a natural, objective standard for good and bad. No guess work by human legislatures is needed.

Thus, nature has an undeniable power in our lives, and the positive law legitimately shares political power with nature. This is self-evident. Positive law determines some things in our lives, but free individuals determine others. And as Locke wrote, these individual decisions must be congruent with right and wrong, i.e., that "the law of nature be observed." [39]

This duality between natural and positive law is evident in our driving of automobiles. Natural law determines where we drive to get our needs met, while positive law determines how fast. Individuals naturally make most decisions. Positive law is in charge of others. Individuals in republics are subject to positive law only when performing regulated or licensed activities.

Given that both natural law and positive law operate in our lives simultaneously, then the only issue for law abiders is to determine the scope of each power's subject matter. That is the

25

object of law. In other words, defining the scope of power is the role of law. In all societies, the primary issue over power is this: Who or what is in charge of what?

There is a name for this dynamic. It is called sovereignty. We have discussed sovereignty since the beginning of this book.

A sovereign is one who has ultimate decision making authority over any particular subject matter. As we are learning, positive law is sovereign over some things while individuals – who answer to nature – are in charge of others.

Because these sovereign jurisdictions are separate; because natural law is opposite, opposed and antecedent to Man's positive law; and because positive law cannot change natural law but must conform to it, then natural law serves as a governor or limiter upon positive law authority.

In the United States, the scope of all natural and positive law power is defined by America's fifty-one constitutions. As these constitutions show us, the scope of natural law is a jurisdictional check upon the authority of positive law.

American constitutions exclude positive law from ruling or adjudicating the subject matter that is under the authority of nature and her natural persons. It is this self-evident duality of law to which Jesus brought our attention.

Two forms of government

As there are two kinds of law (natural and positive law), two kinds of persons (natural and artificial persons), and two kinds of duties (natural law and legal duties), then there are also two forms of national government in this world.

These are 1) the republican form of government and 2) the nonrepublican form of government. Given that the U.S. did not become the world's first federated republic until the ratification of the 14th Amendment, then the ancient republics of Athens and Rome were also only republican prototypes.

Article IV, Section 4 of the U.S. Constitution guarantees

that Congress will provide a republican form of government to the various states, which are themselves republics. As will be explained, republics are characterized by the rule of law, which is to be governed by two sovereigns.

However, most modern national governments in the world are of the nonrepublican form. These include monarchies and dictatorships (the rule by one), oligarchies (the rule by few) and social democracies (the rule by majority). These nonrepublics are characterized by the sole rule of Man.

These two forms of government differ in their 1) number of sovereigns, 2) bases (sources), 3) functions, 4) compositions and 5) structures. This is outlined and introduced immediately below, and is discussed throughout the remainder of this book.

Number of sovereigns. Nonrepublics such as monarchies have one sovereign, e.g., the monarch. Nonrepublics such as social democracies also have one sovereign, i.e., their legislatures. Whether as monarchs or as legislatures, these nonrepublican lawmakers make or create all the law.

Thus, all political duties in a nonrepublic are based on Man's positive law. These sole nonrepublican sovereigns, and the law enforcers and judges that serve them, determine everyone's rights with their written positive law.

In contrast, republics operate under two sovereigns – nature and Man – each with their own legislative and adjudicatory authority over different subject matter. Man's positive law is sovereign over the administration of government, over commercial activities (called commerce), and over foreigners.

In contrast, individuals are in charge of the natural law jurisdiction. This is 1) where they are not bound by contract, and 2) where their free will answers only to nature. We call this power *natural liberty* in the state of nature.

An example of this is the authority that individuals exercise before going to work. In such cases, they get up, use the restroom, exercise, bathe, eat, and brush their teeth without duty to anyone, let alone government. They may also have

27

children to bathe, clothe and feed.. Fulfilling these tasks are their duites that they owe to nature, and their good nature.

Such individuals owe no artificial duties to anyone until they enter their cars to drive to work, which is subject to a motor vehicle code, or until they begin work, which is likely subject to regulatory codes and taxes.

Until then, individuals are free of artificial duties to other people and to their republican governments. Until then, they are fulfilling their natural, mandatory duties before their artificial, consented-to duties begin.

In a republic, positive law is not allowed to legislate over the subject matter that belongs to individuals, which is the exercise of their natural rights and duties. In a republic, individuals have a jurisdiction where they answer only to nature as a sovereign and where they are naturally free of positive law and contractual obligations.

Source / basis. The republican form of government is one which derives its power from its citizens' delegated authority. Republics' authority to create positive law springs from the natural authority of citizens, who delegate some of their political power to government, and yet who retain other power. The power they retain or reserve is the authority to exercise their natural rights, which we call individual sovereignty.

As defined, a sovereign is that person, body or state that maintains ultimate power over any particular subject matter or area. Adult individuals are sovereign over what they eat, over how they spend their money, and over what path that they take home, for example. As we have seen, in this natural jurisdiction, individuals exercise free will subject only to their duties to nature and to those duties to which they have consented.

They do not look to government to make their personal decisions. Nor do they thank government when their bodies properly function. [40] In republics, power is distributed between citizens acting in their natural capacities and the government acting in its artificial capacity. Thus, power is separated

28

between the natural law jurisdiction and the positive law jurisdictions – between the natural authority of individuals and the artificial positive law authority of their governments.

The power granted by citizens to their governments are defined by their constitutions. The 9th and 10th Amendments to the U.S. Constitution say that power not granted to the U.S. government is retained by the states or by individual citizens, who as a group are called *the People*. The People are the group of individual citizens who have constitutionally-reserved natural rights and personal sovereignty. Foreigners are not the People because they are not U.S. citizens, but are instead deportable subjects of Congress.

The U.S. Constitution begins with "We the People...," who are the granters of certain powers to government. That some power is granted to republican governments by the People, and that some power is retained or reserved by the People or their states, are inherent elements of America's republican form of government and federalism. These are key separations of power that we will discuss later.

In contrast, in a nonrepublic there is only one sovereign, i.e., the artificial positive law sovereign – be it a parliament or a monarch. And there is only one kind of recognized law, i.e., positive law, which is whatever the political sovereign dictates.

In a nonrepublic, neither the natural law jurisdiction nor individual sovereignty is recognized, and all of society's authority, criminal standards and political rights are derived from the national artificial sovereign, and not from nature.

Function. Functionally, republics operate as secular governments based on objective and natural standards for crime, citizenship, property ownership, marriage and direct taxation, for example. In contrast, nonrepublics operate as religious governments, based upon supernatural claims of power (by some men over others) and upon subjective, artificial and often arbitrary standards for crime and the rights of subjecthood.

Ultimately, secular justice in republics is based on objec-

29

tive natural science, while justice in nonrepublics is essentially religious – based on belief and opinion.

Composition. Republics are composed of citizens, whose political rights are equal in most respects and who are free unless they consent to be governed, such as by running a regulated business or entering government service. Republics exist to secure the natural political rights of their natural citizens, as well as the granted rights of their adopted citizens.

In contrast, nonrepublics are made up of subjects, or citizen-subjects, of the national sovereign. These subjects' political "rights" are actually privileges. They are neither derived naturally nor are they necessarily equal because they are granted by the artificial sovereign. For example, the sovereign may grant some subjects Titles of Nobility, but not others.

This nonrepublican sovereign imposes its authority by force (based on the principle of might-makes-right) and fraud (based on the false principle, which is contrary to natural law, that some people may determine the political rights of others).

Structure. Structurally, republics are maintained by keeping a separation of powers between their legislative (rule making), judicial (adjudicative) and executive (administrative) branches. However, as we shall see, maintaining America's republics requires keeping a variety of identifiable powers separate, and not just branches of government.

This includes keeping the territorial jurisdiction of the states and Congress separate, keeping the judicial jurisdictions of law and equity separate, keeping regulation separate from criminal prohibition, and keeping the unlimited legislative power of Congress over federal areas, such as the District of Columbia, separate from its limited powers within the states.

In contrast, all subjects, branches and departments of nonrepublics serve only the national legislative sovereign, who is the source and creator of all nonrepublican law. Thus, in nonrepublics, there are no real separations of power and no recognition of natural law or individual sovereignty.

Republics are based on both kinds of law

We have thus established that there are two kinds of law (natural (unwritten) and positive (written) law), two kinds of persons (natural and artificial persons), and two forms of government (republics and nonrepublics). These forms are fundamentally different in that they treat natural and positive law, and natural and artificial persons, differently.

In nonrepublics, all power resides in the sole artificial positive law sovereign, be it a monarch, dictator or legislature, and there is only one kind of recognized law, i.e., positive law. The sovereign is a person or legislative body that claims supernatural power to decree other people's rights and that uses fraud and superior might to maintain this unnatural authority.

Such sole artificial sovereign alone defines its subjects' political rights. This includes their rights of political participation (for example, their right to vote and their non-right to be a king or queen), their rights to be compensated for injury, and the grounds for which individuals may be incarcerated.

In a nonrepublic, neither the power of natural law nor individual sovereignty is recognized, and all of society's authority, criminal standards and political rights are derived from and dictated by the national artificial sovereign – and not by nature.

That is, nonrepublics are based on the denial of nature; of natural standards for crimes, marriage, sex and citizenship; and of the natural law jurisdiction of individuals. In a nonrepublic, Man's usurped and claimed power does not recognize nature's role in defining political rights.

Nonrepublics operate in defiance of natural reality, i.e., that nature is sovereign over some things and that nature makes people politically equal. Given this, for a monarch or nonrepublican legislature to claim unnatural superior authority to define their subjects' rights is to deny natural reality and to usurp nature's political role.

This denial says that some natural persons may create,

31

define and decree the rights and duties of other natural persons. All nonrepublics are based on this false premise or nonsense.

In a nonrepublic, the national artificial political sovereign is the source of all political rights and duties, and all such rights are artificial and subject to the whims of the sovereign. There are no immutable, inherent, unalienable and reserved natural rights, duties or standards in a government that denies natural political law.

Such nonrepublican sovereign secures its sole authority by denying the authority of nature, its equal rights and duties, the legitimacy of its power, and its objective standards.

In contrast with this reliance solely on positive law, the republican form of government is based on both kinds of law – natural and positive law. Republics recognize two sovereigns and two bodies of power – one natural and one artificial.

In a republic, the positive law of the legislature is sovereign over certain subject matter, such as commerce, immigrants and the administration of government, while individual citizens retain or reserve ultimate authority over other subject matter, i.e., the exercise of their natural rights. Thus in republics, there exists the positive law jurisdiction of the political sovereign and the reserved natural law jurisdiction of the People.

In other words, republics respect the natural authority of individuals, which is called individual sovereignty, and this power of individuals is separate from, opposed to, and a check upon the authority of positive law. The artificial, positive law sovereignty of a republican legislature is limited, such that it may not legislate contrary to natural law sovereignty of individuals, which power has been constitutionally reserved.

In a republic, which the U.S. Supreme Court describes as "a government of the people," [41] citizens delegate some of their natural power to government, and they retain the rest. That power which is not delegated to government is individuals' sovereignty over the exercise of their natural reserved constitutional rights, "within the bounds of the law of nature." [42].

Black's Law Dictionary defines natural rights as "those which grow out of (the) nature of man and depend upon his personality and are distinguished from those which are created by positive laws enacted by a duly constituted government to create an orderly civilized society." [43] Given this dictionary recognition, natural rights are undeniable.

The 9th Amendment to the U.S. Constitution says that "(t)he enumeration in the constitution of certain rights shall not be construed to deny or disparage others retained by the people." These "certain rights" are those certain undeniable natural rights that are listed in American constitutions, for example, the rights to life, liberty, property, religion and the pursuit of happiness.

The 9th Amendment says that the writing down of these few "certain rights" is not meant to deny or disparage those others that American constitutions do not write down or mention. Because only natural law need not be written to be effective, the 9th Amendment refers exclusively to natural rights.

These unenumerated natural rights include, among others, the rights of travel, of conscience, of self-defense, of compensation, of ingestion, of intoxication, of inaction, of silence, of representation, and of attraction. They also include the rights to communicate, to value property, to associate with others, to barter, to contract, to alter or abolish government, to be natural born, to be ungoverned without giving consent, to secure the natural born Citizen status of one's offspring, to marry, to be raised and cared for, and to migrate. [44] And as we shall also see, everyone in the world has a natural universal right to a republican form of government, but few know this.

All-in-all, the exercise of natural rights involve activities for which none of us look to government to determine for us. For example, no one looks to their king or their legislature to tell them what and when to eat, when and how long to sleep, who to like, or what to buy at a hardware or grocery store.

That individuals have these reserved natural rights is

33

expressed by the Indiana Supreme Court in *Beebe v. State* (1855) where the Court upheld the natural right of individuals to possess alcohol.

Note below that the Court 1) echoes the 13th Amendment and Article I, Section 37 of the Indiana Constitution, i.e., that liberty is guaranteed unless one commits a crime, and 2) echoes the *Declaration of Independence,* i.e., that governments are "instituted among Men" to secure people's natural rights.

> "Under our constitution, then, we all have some rights that have not been surrendered, which are consequently reserved, and which government can not deprive us of unless we shall first forefeit them by our crimes; and to secure to us the enjoyment of those rights is the great aim and end of the constitution itself." [45]

In republics, individuals operate in two capacities. They function in a sovereign natural law capacity and, if they choose, in a positive law capacity. When acting in their natural law capacity, such as doing laundry, cutting their own grass, or washing the dishes, individuals operate as natural persons. In such capacity, they are not directly subject to government and its regulations. Nor are these taxable activities.

In contrast, acting in their positive law capacity, such as selling fruits and vegetables, operating a professional lawn service, or washing dishes at a restaurant, individuals operate as commercial, artificial persons who are subject to governments' taxation and regulation. All individuals who derive income from commerce with the public are operating in their artificial capacities under positive law authority, subject to a legislature.

This is true in both nonrepublics and in America's republics. Both republican and nonrepublican legislatures are sovereign over commerce, which is to derive income from selling goods or services to the public.

So, in a republic, the legislature has a jurisdiction that is separate from the jurisdiction of individuals, and individuals naturally operate within the natural law jurisdiction unless they voluntarily enter the positive law jurisdiction of the legislature. By entering this artificial positive law authority, for example by selling fruits and vegetables for profit, then individuals give their consent authority to be governed by a legislature.

To exit the natural law jurisdiction of gardening and to enter the positive law jurisdiction of selling fruits and vegetables to the public is to give government one's consent authority to be regulated or ruled in some fashion. This consent authority is referred to in the *Declaration of Independence*.

It says that governments derive "their just powers from the consent of the governed..." So, when an individual enters the world of commerce, for example, then that person consents to be governed as an artificial person. This is to become subject to government's regulation.

Conversely, as we shall see, republican governments are illegitimate when acting upon natural persons without their explicit or implied consent.

This literally means that unless Americans explicitly or tacitly give their consent to be regulated by the commercial or administrative jurisdictions of government, such as by the motor vehicle regime or the income tax system, then they would be naturally free of government. In other words, if one does not drive a car or earn income, for example, then one is not subject to a motor vehicle code or the income tax system.

Thus in republics, individual sovereigns are born free of and ungoverned by positive law unless they voluntarily enter its jurisdiction and consent to be governed by its authority. They are sovereign and free until they voluntarily enter the scope of government where they may be taxed and regulated.

If Americans do not drive motor vehicle or earn income, then they are free of the income tax and licensing systems. Nothing says that babies will grow up to be automobile drivers or income taxpayers. Nature pushes us only to grow up and old.

Babies – and other living things – naturally owe no duties to their republican governments. When they grow up, they naturally owe duties only to other people, such as the duty to not harm them. The duties that they owe to republican governments are only by consent, which is to voluntarily enter governments' positive law police power of regulation.

We will learn later how natural born Citizens are particularly free of government. This is because they are born free of it. Such citizens consent to be governed only by entering government's positive law authority. Otherwise, such natural law citizens are not and never have been subject to positive law at all.

Of course they owe other people natural duties, but they are naturally born free of artificial duties imposed by their republican governments. These latter legal duties are imposed upon natural persons who are acting in an artificial capacity and who have thus consented to legislative authority.

Likewise, as we shall see, when a person enters a federal area such as the District of Columbia, then that person consents to be governed by Congress in a different capacity than Congress normally treats people within the states. Within the American states, Congress is to treat people as would a republic.

Within the states, Congress owes state citizens a republican form of government, including due process of law. However, when these same citizens enters a federal area, then they consent to be governed by Congress as artificial persons in a nonrepublican manner, as if they were in Great Britain.

The opposite is also true. Unless one enters governmental service, or unless one participates in commerce and subjects oneself to regulation, or unless one exits a state and enters a federal area, such as an airliner, then that person acts in his or her natural / non-artificial capacity. In such role, one is free of all government, except natural self-government and the laws of nature, including its natural prohibitions of torts and crimes.

This consent process to the equity jurisdiction is voluntary. It is voluntary because citizens do not have to enter the positive law jurisdiction of government unless they chose to, and because they have other choices. For example, people can choose to earn income to purchase food, or they can choose to produce their own food. The former is subject to taxation and regulation. Short of being a nuisance, the latter generally is not.

This consent process in a republic is moral to the extent that people, and particularly citizens, 1) know that they are exiting nature's jurisdiction and entering a positive law authority of government, and 2) know the consequences of entering the positive law jurisdiction, such as to know their artificial duties.

Thus, in a republic, unless individuals give their voluntary consent to be governed as artificial persons in a positive law jurisdiction of government, then they are naturally ungoverned, or free of government. The artificial positive law jurisdiction of republican governments is always voluntarily entered.

The power to consent comes from one's natural law authorty, which we have called free will. One consents to the equity jurisdiction by registering with regulators or by engaging in regulated activities. Otherwise, one is naturally free of duty to positive law, and one only owes natural duties to other people.

Whereas this positive law jurisdiction is voluntarily entered with one's consent, in contrast the natural law jurisdiction is compulsory and inescapable. Treating others with a degree of respect, by not threatening or harming them, is at all times mandatory under natural political law.

Thus, nature's jurisdiction and the physical and political duties that it imposes are not subject to consent. Natural political law defines what is right and wrong wherever people go.

So when someone violates a natural rule, such as the natural prohibition against murder, then the criminal jurisdiction is compulsory. This is because the duty to not murder is mandatory, and because the natural laws of compensation and retribution require justice. Harming others invokes the physical, cognitive, emotional and political laws of nature.

One does not consent to natural justice because we are

37

naturally always subject to our natural duties. In a republic, people consent only to positive law because it is an artificial authority into which they are not naturally born and bound.

Likewise, natural people do not have to invoke positive law to gain natural justice. As we shall see, rendering natural justice and adjudicating natural law is the role of the law jurisdiction of American judicial courts, whose authority and due process of law are not subject to the positive law of legislatures.

In a republic, torts and crimes are naturally proscribed as *malum in se* – wrong by their injurious nature – regardless of the wishes of legislators. Legislatures may prescribe (write down) what nature proscribes (prohibits), and may affix penalties for such harmful behavior. However, republican legislatures have no authority to legislate (create or abolish) natural duties, whose breaches are torts or crimes.

Natural duties, such as to care for one's children and to defend the homeland in event of invasion, operate outside of positive law. Legislatures do not legislate (create) such duties. They merely write them down when appropriate.

Although these duties get codified in code books, and although legislatures assign penalties for their violations, the existence of these duties is not subject to positive law. Legislatures cannot turn our natural duties to one another on and off. Nor have they any delegated authority from citizens to invent or create crimes that do not include injury, or to treat real crimes, which are injurious behaviors, as noncriminal.

For example, a legislature may not waive parents' duty to care for their children, or people's duty to not steal from others. This is because positive law does not create these natural duties in people and because, by definition, positive law does not apply to natural persons doing natural wrongs, called *malum in se.*

In contrast, republican legislatures only have authority to create legal rights, which are state-granted privileges for artificial persons. Artificial persons owe all their positive law, legal powers and duties to their legislative sovereign, which not only created the artificial persons, but also defined their attributes. For example, S- and C-corporations have only the characteristics, powers and duties that legislatures decree.

Unless natural persons breach a natural duty, or unless they exit the natural law jurisdiction and consent to be regulated by a positive law authority, then adult individuals are not governed in republics. This means that they are free of government and the rule of others 1) unless they violate natural law by committing *malum in se*, or 2) unless they consent to be regulated under legitimate power that citizens have granted to to their governments.

As we have seen, republican legislatures have authority to write down or codify natural rights and duties for natural persons, but legislatures do not create (or legislate) such rights and duties. Thus, in republics, positive law may not be used to violate people's natural rights because legislatures may not legislate over such rights.

As the Indiana Supreme Court wrote in *Beebe v. State* (1855): "There are certain absolute rights ... which, in all free governments, must of necessity be protected from legislative interference..." [46] These are "rights that have not been surrendered, which are consequently reserved, and which government can not deprive us of unless we shall first forefeit them by our crimes," wrote the Court [47]

The Supremacy Clause of the U.S. Constitution at Article VI, Clause 2, as well as the Supremacy Clauses in state constitutions, say that such constitutions are the supreme law in the United States. Because of this, all statutes must be consistent with them. [48]

This requires judicial courts to use the meaning of cases, crimes, offenses, felonies and misdemeanors as they are referred to in American constitutions to include injury. Otherwise, the legislative sovereign could subjectively and arbitrarily determine who belongs in jail.

Thus, American republics secure their citizens' natural

rights by adhering to the inherent meanings given to said words by American constitutions. Relying on the natural constitutional definitions of these words is a substantive right, just like all of the rights in the Bill of Rights.

For example, the 13th Amendment to the U.S. Constitution says that slavery is prohibited except as punishment for the commission of crime. This is also what the *Beebe* Court said: that people's natural rights are unalienable "unless we shall first forefeit them by our crimes." [49]

These references to crime are to the constitutional meaning of crime, which always includes injury. Criminal cases are subject to the Case or Controversy Requirement of Article III, Section 2 of the U.S. Constitution, which requires injury-in-fact.

In a republic, because case and crime are defined objectively – as a violation of natural law – then people may be enslaved only for harming others. Says the 6th Amendment, this is subject to the judgment of a jury of one's peers. In other words, it is only an injury that puts a criminal case *in jury*.

Otherwise, if American legislatures could redefine crime unnaturally, then that power would necessarily violate the 13th Amendment. In such a case, legislative majorities could put disfavored people in jail for whatever reason they chose, such as for the possession of certain property or for the operation of unwanted businesses.

Likewise, because each branch of republican government gains its power from a constitution, then without a constitutional amendment, the branches' powers cannot be changed or enlarged. Said another way: to change the branches' separations of power requires a constitutional amendment.

This means that republican legislatures lack authority to expand the criminal law jurisdiction of judicial courts. Republican legislatures may only create non-criminal legal duties in artificial persons that they have created and that have consented to their artificial authority.

Equally important in a republic is that positive law exists

to secure the operation of natural law, the natural rights of individuals, and individual sovereignty. "It is to secure our rights that we resort to government at all," wrote Thomas Jefferson. [50]

The *Declaration of Independence*, which Jefferson wrote, also says this: that to secure people's natural rights is the reason that governments are instituted (created). This includes securing the role of nature in determining wrong from right and what is criminal from what is allowed by the political laws of nature.

Thus, republics are based on the respect for natural law and natural standards, which define such things as crimes, rights to property and natural citizenship, and which are not subject to inconsistent legislation. Republican legislatures have no authority to define people's natural political rights as artificial rights, i.e., coming from an artificial sovereign.

Republican legislatures may not legislate over nature, or try to legislate over human nature, because individuals have not consented to their authority. Nonrepublics deny nature's power to define such things as crime and citizenship, so as to claim such power for Man.

Nonrepublics cannot exist in an environment where the judiciary recognizes, knows and upholds the natural source of right and wrong. This unalterable source of law is nature, instead of whimsical, subjective and arbitrary Man.

Nonrepublics are incompatible with and antagonistic to natural law, whose role they must deny to avoid admitting their own illegitimacy. That is, if people realized that their rights come from nature, then they would not look to a king, a legislature or a court to grant such rights.

And if people realized that all their natural political rights are equal, then they would know 1) that kings and legislatures have no authority to determine their rights, which are natural facts, and 2) that kings and legislatures maintain such power only by force and fraud (the intentional misrepresentation of republican law as having only an artificial sovereign).

41

Individual sovereignty

The following quotation from *Yick Wo v. Hopkins* (1886) is how the U.S. Supreme Court beautifully described individual sovereignty.

> "Sovereignty itself is, of course, not subject to law, for it is the author and source of law; but in our system, while sovereign powers are delegated to the agencies of government, sovereignty itself remains with the people, by whom and for whom all government exists and acts. And the law is the definition and limitation of power. It is indeed, quite true, that there must always be lodged somewhere, and in some person or body, the authority of final decision; and in many cases of mere administration the responsibility is purely political, no appeal except to the ultimate tribunal of the public judgement, exercised either in the pressure of opinion or by means of the suffrage. But the fundamental rights to life, liberty, and the pursuit of happiness, considered as individual possessions, are secured by those maxims of constitutional law which are the monuments showing the victorious progress of the race in securing to men the blessings of civilization under the reign of just and equal laws, so that, in the famous language of the Massachusetts Bill of Rights, the government of the commonwealth "may be a government of laws and not of men." For, the very idea that one man may be compelled to hold his life, or the means of living, or any material right essential to the enjoyment of life, at the mere will of another, seems to be intolerable in any country where freedom prevails, as being the essence of slavery itself." [51]

Rarely can one find such a marvelous, all encompassing statement of law as the above quotation from the U.S. Supreme

Court. It says several things that are relevant and important to our discussion. (All of the unreferenced quotations below are from the above longer quotation.)

First, the Supreme Court says that sovereignty is the "authority of final decision" which "must always be lodged somewhere, and in some person or body." This is the perfect definition of sovereignty.

Law in a republic is about divvying-up this "authority of final decision." In this book I define this sovereignty in terms of legislative and subject matter jurisdiction. I frame sovereignty in terms of who may legislate over and who may adjudicate various subject matter.

As we shall see, individual sovereigns have "authority of final decision" in all non-injurious personal matters. The judicial branch has "authority of final decision" over cases involving injury and in appellate matters. The legislative and executive branches, which are called the political branches, have "authority of final decision" over commerce, immigration, and governmental affairs, for instance.

Each of these entities in America's republics, i.e., individuals and the three branches of government, are sovereign over separate subject matter assigned to them, or in the case of individual sovereigns, retained by them. This, of course, is because "sovereignty itself remains with the people" in a republic. Sovereignty remains with the people because they delegate some but not all of their natural authority to government.

Second, the Supreme Court says that the source of all sovereignty is the people. This necessarily implies that Congress, which derived its power from the people, occupies a subordinate status to the people's sovereignty. This is because individual sovereignty is unalienable, and is unassailable to the power of positive law. Power that is not "delegated to the agencies of government" "remains with the people."

Third, the Supreme Court says that "law is the definition and limitation of power." The law defines power, which is

43

another word for jurisdiction. Power not delegated by the people is a limitation upon government's jurisdiction.

For example, power not granted to judicial courts over non-injury is a limitation on the courts' subject matter jurisdiction over things that are regulated. Good law enforcement always first defines the "authority of final decision."

Fourth, the Supreme Court says that it is the people "by whom and for whom all government exists and acts." This expresses that the nation's founders created the positive law of government to serve the people, not to preside over them.

Fifth, the Supreme Court distinguishes "the fundamental rights to life, liberty, and the pursuit of happiness" from those matters that are "purely political" and subject only "to the ultimate tribunal of the public judgement..." This recognizes that natural rights are not subject to politics, religion or legislation.

Sixth, the Supreme Court says that one's rights to life, liberty and the pursuit of happiness are "considered as individual possessions." These rights belong to each of us because they do not belong to anyone else.

Seventh, the Supreme Court says that slavery occurs when "any material right essential to the enjoyment of life," such as the right of property possession or the right of liberty, is "at the mere will of another." [52] Being subject to the will of others is "intolerable in any country where freedom prevails, as being the essence of slavery itself."

This is to say that when the executive and judicial branches deprive natural persons of their liberty based on "the mere will of" the legislature, instead of nature's criminal standards, then this is a condition of slavery. This is to say that "any material right essential to the enjoyment of life," such as property possession and use, is not subject to the "mere will of another."

The eighth and most important lesson for us in *Yick Wo v. Hopkins* (1886) is that individual sovereignty "is, of course, not subject to law, for it is the author and source of law."

Hmmmm, did you read the above quotation correctly? The Supreme Court plainly says that individual sovereigns in America are "not subject to law." Can this be so? The answer is:

Without acknowledging the natural law jurisdiction in the U.S. Constitution, wherein nature is sovereign, then the above Supreme Court statement is not really comprehensible. In fact, without understanding the role of natural law in a republic, then crime and citizenship are not comprehensible.

Without knowledge of natural law, which such knowledge the Court in *Yick Wo v. Hopkins* (1886) exhibits, or without acknowledging the existence of a law other than positive law, then one must take the above statement literally, i.e., that individual sovereignty is not subject to law.

But of course individuals are subject to law. The world does not revolve around them. Regardless of government, individuals are naturally and normally subject to the laws of nature, including its criminal standards.

Americans are just not naturally and normally subject to the positive law of government. This means that the above Supreme Court statement is only properly understood as:

"(Natural) sovereignty itself is, of course, not subject to (positive) law, for it is the author and source of (positive) law."

Because "the law is the definition and limitation of power," [53] then the people created the positive law to define and limit the positive law authority of government. Republics are limited in power in that they may not legitimately encroach upon the natural law jurisdiction of individuals, who are not born subject to the positive law power of the equity jurisdiction.

In the law jurisdiction, individuals have primary subject matter jurisdiction over their own personal affairs. This personal jurisdiction is outside and superior to positive law, but cannot escape the duties imposed by the political aws of nature.

Natural law citizens and positive law citizens

As we have learned, there are two sources of recognized power in a republic, i.e., nature and the national political sovereign. Respectively these are the sources of natural law and positive law, each which has its own authority over separate subject matter.

In contrast, nonrepublics recognize only one source of people's rights, i.e., the positive law of the political sovereign. This sovereign has plenary authority over all subject matter, human subjects, and land, air and water. In a nonrepublic, individuals are born subject to the positive law authority of this sovereign. These people are called subjects, or citizen-subjects.

Such nonrepublican sovereign defines its subjects' political rights, including whether or not they qualify to be the sovereign. They don't. Particularly in a monarchy, only the monarch can pass-on political sovereignty through natural reproduction, and only a natural offspring of a monarch has an inherited political right to be the chief political leader of the country.

The sovereign does not recognize any such equal natural jurisdiction in his subjects or citizen-subjects. All of their political power is strictly artificial. Their political power has been granted by the political sovereign himself, who has unnaturally claimed the authority to grant such power.

The *Magna Carta* (1215) is a case in point. While it is recognized as an important milestone in the achievement of rights for mankind, the only rights achieved were positive law, legal rights – granted by King John of England.

It was not for another 560 years, when the American colonies' declared independence from King George of England, that government was reborn (from ancient Mediterranean prototypes) to recognize people's natural rights, which equality of rights is opposite and opposed to the principles of all nonrepublics.

In contrast to nonrepublics, where all citizen-subjects

have their political rights granted by positive law, the republican form of government has two kinds of citizens. Republics have 1) natural law citizens, whose political rights are created through natural reproduction and inherited under natural law, and 2) positive law citizens, whose rights are granted under a sovereign's positive law authority of naturalization. Article I, Section 8, Clause 4 of the U.S. Constitution grants Congress power to "establish an uniform Rule of naturalization..."

Republics have two kinds of citizens because there are two sovereigns in a republic (nature and Man), and there are two types of law that operate at all times (natural law and positive law). These two kinds of citizens are analogous to children in a family, who are either natural born or adopted.

This means that republics have both 1) natural citizens who are created under natural law through natural sexual reproduction (just like kings and queens are), and 2) artificial citizens who are created (or adopted) by positive law, as are all citizen-subjects in nonrepublics. Thus, a key difference between republics and nonrepublics is that the former recognize natural law citizens, who are not created or adopted by positive law.

In the United States, natural law citizens are called *natural born Citizens*. They are natural law citizens of the states in the union. In contrast, positive law citizens, who are adopted at birth or after birth under the authority of the 14th Amendment, are called *Citizens of the United States*.

In republics, natural law citizens are not created by or born under the jurisdiction of positive law, but instead are born into the natural political jurisdiction of their fathers, whose natural acts of claiming and reporting their children secure these offsprings' membership in the political society.

"By the law of nature alone, children follow the condition of their fathers, and enter into all their rights;" wrote Swiss legal philosopher Emerich de Vattel in *The Law of Nations, or The Principles of the Law of Nature Applied to Nations and Sovereigns (1758).* [54] "(T)he place of birth produces no change in this

47

particular, and cannot of itself furnish any reason for taking from a child what nature has given him..."

Thus, it is solely by "the law of nature alone" that a natural law citizen obtains all his or her political rights in a republic. This status is achieved through a natural claiming process by citizen fathers. "(M)ales secure their children's natural right to citizenship by their own testimony," explained Paul A. Guthrie in *Demonic Positivism*. This is "because males have no natural way to rely upon any witness to prove their paternity..." [55]

Unlike with mothers, whose pregnancy and birthing can be witnessed, fathers must actually claim their children because there are no witnesses to their fatherhood. This natural claiming process is accomplished 1) by marriage to the child's mother or 2) by oath, affirmation or legitimation. Legitimation is a codified testimonial process to place "a child born out of wedlock in the same legal position as a child born in wedlock." [56]

"As the society cannot exist and perpetuate itself otherwise than by the children of the citizens, those children naturally follow the conditions of their fathers, and succeed to all their rights...," wrote Vattel. "The country of the fathers is therefore that of the children; and these become true citizens merely by their tacit consent."

As we have seen, it is by a deliberate act that individuals exit the natural law jurisdiction and enter the positive law jurisdiction of equity in a republic. For example, we apply for Social Security numbers, drivers licenses and building permits. However, Vattel tells us that natural law citizens tacitly consent to society's political jurisdiction, and that no deliberate act by the child is necessary to secure the child's citizenship.

Thus, under the U.S. Constitution, America's natural law citizens tacitly consent to the natural law jurisdiction of the political society, which enforces their political rights and duties. Under this arrangement, they need not consent to be governed by Congress' positive law authority, and are therefore born free of Congress' power. This is what makes them free.

"(D)ue to reproductive biological differences, the mother is naturally dependent upon the natural political act of the father in order to secure political rights for her offspring as natural political rights," writes Guthrie. [57] In the absence of a citizen father, the mother looks to the sovereign of her nation or of the place of the child's birth to claim the child as a citizen.

Such adopted citizens are positive law citizens who gain their citizenship rights from a national political sovereign. This citizenship is based on non-fatherly criteria such as the nationality of the mother and the place of birth.

All positive law citizenship, as codified by the 14th Amendment, is based on either *jus sanguinis* (the principle that citizenship is determined by the citizenship of one's parents) or *jus soli* (the principle that citizenship is determined by one's place of birth).

Both natural born Citizens and (naturalized) Citizens of the United States are referred to as separate proper nouns at Article II, Section 1, Clause 5 of the U.S. Constitution, which reads: "No Person except a natural born Citizen, or a Citizen of the United States, at the time of the Adoption of this constitution, shall be eligible to that Office who shall not have attained to the Age of thirty five Years, and been fourteen Years a Resident within the United States."

This provision, called the natural born Citizen clause, is significant for several reasons. First, it naturalized or adopted all state citizens within the American colonies "at the time of the Adoption of this constitution" and made them Citizens of the United States. Prior to the ratification of the U.S. Constitution, all state citizens were foreign subjects (alien to the U.S.), and thus had to be naturalized to become U.S. citizens.

Second, the provision grandfathers-in the right of these adopted citizens "at the time of the Adoption of this constitution" to be President. Thereafter, once all of these original adopted citizens had died, then only natural born Citizens, who are the offspring U.S. citizens, could serve as U.S. President.

As soon as the U.S. Constitution was ratified, and prior to Congress ever even meeting, these new Citizens of the United States were busy creating natural born Citizens through natural reproduction. These new Citizens of the United States did not need Congress either 1) to meet or 2) to define the rights of their citizenship, including their exclusive right to make future U.S. Presidents. Properly understood, the above Article II, Section 1, Clause 5 of the U.S. Constitution secured these rights for them.

Third, the provision also means that natural born Citizens are not Citizens of the United States. Within the state republics, both are mutually exclusive kinds of U.S. citizens. Nowhere in the U.S. Constitution or in U.S. statutes (that I have found) are these two kinds of citizens equated.

All U.S. citizens are either natural born Citizens or they are adopted Citizens of the United States, but not both. Members of Congress, at a minimum, are to be Citizens of the United States, with certain age and residency requirements. [58]

The U.S. Constitution is a social contract with U.S. citizens. It is not a contract with foreign (alien) citizens. Thus, the constitution does not secure for alien fathers a right to convey natural U.S. citizenship upon their offspring through marriage, oath, affirmation or legitimation, as it does U.S. citizen fathers.

This makes all offspring born from foreign fathers naturally alien to the United States. "A Nation, or the sovereign who represents it, may confer citizenship upon an alien and admit him into the body politic," wrote Vattel. "This act is called naturalization." [59] Similarly Bouvier's Dictionary (1856) defines naturalization as "(t)he act by which an alien is made a Citizen of the United States of America." [60] Thus, all Citizens of the United States are adopted natural-aliens to the United States.

This constitutional term always refers to an adopted, non-natural law U.S. citizen. Bouvier defines a naturalized citizen as: "One who, being born an alien, has lawfully become a Citizen of the United States under the constitution and laws." [61]

So, natural born aliens – who are children born to foreign

or unknown fathers – may be adopted by the 14th Amendment. It adopts all aliens born on U.S. soil and all who Congress makes eligible for naturalization. In general, Congress adopts or naturalizes at birth all alien children who are born to qualified U.S. mothers anywhere in the world. [62]

However, the constitution does not grant Congress power to define or to create natural born Citizens, which are facts of nature, created through natural reproduction, secured through marriage, oath, affirmation or legitimation, defined by their D.N.A., [63] and born outside of Congress' legislative authority.

Natural born Citizenship is secured and established by U.S citizen fathers under their reserved natural law authority in the U.S. Constitution, and not under the delegated legislative positive-law authority of Congress.

While U.S. courts may revoke naturalized citizenship if it is acquired by fraud, Congress may not revoke one's natural born Citizenship, which it did not grant. *Steinkauler's Case* (circa 1875), [64] cited in *Perkins v. Elg* (1939), [65] shows that such natural born Citizenship is unrevocable and unalienable.

If a right is unalienable and unrevocable by an act of Congress or by the judiciary, then such natural born Citizenship is a natural political right. It is a natural political right just as are individuals' rights to life, liberty, property and the pursuit of happiness, which are also unassailable by legislatures.

Once aliens or their offspring become adopted U.S. citizens, either at birth or after birth, then such citizens' natural political rights to vote, to run for political office, and to create natural born Citizens are recognized. Such adopted citizens have all the political rights of natural born Citizens except for the natural right to run for President or Vice President.

According to *Bouvier's Law Dictionary* (1856), a Citizen of the United States "has all the rights of a natural born Citizen except that of being eligible as president or vice-president of the United States." [66]

Because natural born Citizenship is a natural inherited

right, this means that to run for President or Vice President is also a natural inherited right, and one to be exercised only by natural law citizens. Thus, the right to run for the presidency is not a legal right granted by positive law, i.e., the 14th Amendment, as a privilege of being adopted.

This means that Congress cannot legislate over the right to be President, which right comes only from the natural law jurisdiction of U.S. fathers, which is not subject to an inconsistent Congress. Congress has no authority to grant the offspring of foreign fathers the natural right to run for U.S. President, which the U.S. Constitution reserves only for the products of U.S. citizen fathers under natural political law.

Again, Congress may not and generally does not try to legislate inconsistently with citizens' natural political rights. In America's republics, such rights include not only the natural rights to life, liberty, property, religion and the pursuit of happiness, but also 1) the natural right of all U.S. citizens to have a natural born Citizen President, 2) the natural right of natural born Citizens to exclusively be U.S. Presidents, 3) the natural right of all male U.S. citizens – both male natural born Citizens and male Citizens of the United States – to be the sole source of U.S. Presidents, and 4) the natural right of mothers to choose the nationality of their children via their choice of fathers.

Thus, Presidents need not have U.S. citizen mothers, and except in cases of rape, U.S. mothers chose the nationality of their children. Converse-ly, U.S. citizens whose citizenship is based solely upon their mother's U.S. nationality or upon their birth on U.S. soil may not run for U.S. President. This is because such offspring are adopted citizens who have alien or unknown fathers. For more information, see footnote. [67]

Prior to the American revolution, kings were the only political sovereigns from whom political sovereignty could be inherited. However, in the *Declaration of Independence* the nation's founders declared that "all Men are created equal," each with political sovereignty equal to that of kings.

This included being equally endowed by their Creator to secure political sovereignty for their offspring through natural reproduction, just like a king. This expression of individual political sovereignty and natural political equality is the bedrock of America's republican form of government and its natural law citizens. Without a natural law basis in both its citizenry and Presidents, the U.S. republic ceases to operate.

Natural law in U.S. citizenship statutes

As we shall see below, Congress' citizenship statutes recognize the republican form of government's two varieties of citizens and the two jurisdictions, i.e., natural law and positive law, from which these citizens and their rights derive.

For example, 8 USC 1409 explains the citizenship of children born out of wedlock, outside of the territorial United States – in a virtual state of nature. Under this statute, the children born to unwed U.S. fathers are treated differently (and more harshly) than children born to unwed U.S. mothers.

For instance, 8 USC 1409(a) requires unwed U.S. fathers 1) to prove their blood relationship with such children, 2) to prove their own U.S. nationality, and 3) to promise to care for the child until age eighteen. Then the father must a) legitimate the child under the law of the child's residence, b) acknowledge in writing under oath his paternity, or c) establish his paternity by adjudication in a competent court.

On the other hand, 8 USC 1409(c) requires no such action by U.S. mothers to create U.S. citizens out of wedlock in foreign countries with foreign mates. This citizenship occurs by operation of positive law. 8 USC 1409(c) says that Congress bestows U.S. citizenship upon the offspring of unmarried U.S. mothers who meet a U.S. residency requirement.

This disparity in treatment between the offspring of the two sexes of U.S. citizens has nonetheless been upheld by the U.S. Supreme Court in *Nguyen v. I.N.S.* (2001) as consistent with the 14th Amendment's Equal Protection Clause. [68] This is 1) because the statute is consistent with natural law, which defines natural born Citizenship, and 2) because the types of citizenship discussed at 8 USC 1409(a) and (c) are different.

In the state of nature, the parenthood of citizen mothers is self-proving and witnessable. The witnesses for birth certificates attest to the identity of a child's mother.

However, there are no witnesses in the state of nature to the natural parenthood of fathers. Even witnessing a sex act does not guarantee that a man is the natural father of a child. This naturally requires the father to step forward and claim his children as his own.

As mentioned earlier, this natural claiming process by men is accomplished in one of two fashions. The U.S. father claims his offspring as U.S. citizens either: 1) by marrying the mother, or 2) by oath, adjudication or legitimation.

This claiming of offspring out of wedlock in foreign countries is accomplished by U.S. citizen fathers under 8 USC 1409(a). It defines the steps that U.S. fathers must take to secure the citizenship of their children born out of wedlock and outside of their country.

Males must perform these procedures because under natural law there are no witnesses to or proof of their fatherhood. Thus, 8 USC 1409(a) is not positive law, but instead codified natural law – just as are crimes in republican code books.

8 USC 1409(a) shows 1) that the citizenship of children born of U.S. fathers is not a bestowed privilege from Congress, but instead the result of the actions of U.S. fathers, and 2) that natural citizenship is not achieved automatically at birth, by operation of positive law, under Congress' powers of naturalization. (Natural law citizenship that is proven through oath, adjudication or legitimation relates back to birth.)

This means that citizenship granted under 8 USC 1409(a) is not naturalized citizenship. Instead, Congress looks to the citizen father, who has primary jurisdiction over the natural citizenship of the child, to claim or legitimate the child as a U.S. citizen during the child's first eighteen years.

In contrast, in the case of a child born abroad to an eligible unwed U.S. mother, 8 USC 1409(c) shows that this child is a naturalized U.S. citizen at birth. This is because Congress bestows citizenship upon that child due to the U.S. nationality of the mother, which Congress may do under its powers of naturalization. Such adopted naturalized children are Citizens of the United States.

This means that Congress looks first to the U.S. citizen father to establish natural law citizenship for the child. This is so to not violate the natural jurisdiction of U.S. fathers under the U.S. Constitution. This power is to secure the natural political rights of their children as natural born Citizens, eligible to be U.S. President.

And thus, U.S. fathers have primary and exclusive jurisdiction over natural citizenship. This natural right is so superior to Congress' positive law authority that Congress waits eighteen years for a U.S. father to exercise his natural authority.

If an unwed U.S. father fails to properly secure his foreign born child's citizenship through marriage, oath or legitimation, then the power of the father to convey natural citizenship can lapse. This was upheld in *Nguyen v. I.N.S.* (2001). [69]

Ultimately, under codified natural law at 8 USC 1409(a), the U.S. government defers to the natural source of natural law citizens, i.e., U.S. fathers, to create natural born Citizens. However, when the father fails through either marriage or other affirmative acts to secure his offsprings' natural rights in the political society, then Congress awards naturalized citizenship, which is artificial positive law citizenship, based upon the mother's U.S. nationality.

Unlike U.S. fathers who may only produce natural born Citizens, U.S. mothers have the exclusive power to give birth to either natural born Citizens or naturalized Citizens of the United States, depending upon their choice of fathers. This means that, except in cases of involuntary rape, U.S. mothers completely control the citizenship of their children.

They can choose to bear children with U.S. fathers to create natural born Citizens, who can run for U.S. President. Or they can choose to bear children with alien fathers to create naturalized U.S. citizens. U.S. fathers do not have this choice.

Thus, whereas U.S. males have the plenary power to secure the natural citizenship of their children, they can only secure natural citizenship. However, U.S. mothers have the plenary power to decide both the nationality of their children, as well as the type of U.S. citizenship that their children receive.

Whereas U.S. mothers secure the natural born Citizenship for their children only by marrying U.S. citizen fathers, U.S. fathers secure the natural born Citizenship of their offspring through marriage or through other affirmative acts.

Thus, both U.S. mothers and U.S. fathers have equal natural political rights to create natural born Citizens. However, because of men's and women's natural differences, they secure the natural law citizenship of their children differently.

For mothers who want their children to run for U.S. President, it is imperative to be impregnated by a male U.S. citizen. It also helps to marry him. All legitimate U.S. Presidents and Vice Presidents have the D.N.A. of U.S. citizen fathers. The offspring of these U.S. fathers have a natural, constitutionally-secured claim upon the nation's highest office.

The children of foreign fathers naturally do not. This is because foreign fathers are not parties to the U.S. Constitution. This is also because artificial, adopted U.S. citizens cannot naturally or fully represent the interests of natural ones.

Therefore, U.S. citizenship law shows the operation of the natural law jurisdiction and the positive law jurisdiction of the U.S. Constitution. U.S. citizen fathers are in charge of securing their children's inherited natural political rights under natural law. This natural right of citizen fathers is not created, but only codified by the U.S. Constitution and by Congress at 8

USC 1409(a).

In the absence of a U.S. father, the 14th Amendment looks 1) to the child's birth on U.S. soil, or 2) to Congress' naturalization statutes to determine if the child has been adopted at birth as a Citizen of the United States. Congress grants naturalization at birth to children born to U.S. mothers who have resided in the U.S. In the absence of these circumstances, a foreign person may apply for naturalization after birth.

All such naturalized Citizens of the United States – whether or not naturalized at birth – share one characteristic. Every single one of them has a foreign father. Because these fathers are not parties to the U.S. Constitution, then the constitution does not secure their right to be the source of natural born Citizens, and thus to be a source of U.S. Presidents.

Consequently, for example, no king from any country may sire a child to be born on U.S. soil or to a U.S. mother, who can then be both U.S. President and a king. By definition, all U.S. citizens who have foreign fathers are naturalized Citizens of the United States and are not eligible to be U.S. President.

To conclude this section, we have established 1) that there is a natural law jurisdiction and a positive law jurisdiction in the U.S. and state constitutions, 2) that natural born Citizens are U.S. citizens who are born into the natural political law jurisdiction of their U.S. fathers, and are not adopted by the positive law jurisdiction of the United States, and 3) that natural born Citizens' political rights are equal natural rights, derived from nature and not from positive law.

This essentially means that natural born Citizens are U.S. citizens who are born free of Congress – outside of Congress' positive law authority. In contrast, naturally-foreign and adopted Citizens of the United States are beholden to positive law, which granted them their political rights.

Naturalized citizenship is a privilege bestowed by positve law, and subject to some legal duty to Congress. On the other hand, natural born Citizens are born without duty to Congress.

Delegation of citizens' natural political power

As we have seen, in nonrepublics there are only artificial persons and artificial citizen-subjects whose rights are granted by the sole artificial political sovereign. In contrast, in republics, whose constitutions have both a natural and positive law jurisdiction, called the law and equity jurisdictions, government recognizes both natural and artificial persons, natural and artificial citizens, and natural and artificial rights and duties.

In republics, positive law is to serve natural law. Thus, positive law may not be inconsistent with any of the physical, cognitive, emotional and political laws of nature. For example, when the *Declaration of Independence* says that we are all naturally born equal, this means that none of us are naturally born subject to anyone else, such as a king, a plantation owner, a neighbor or a legislature.

It also means that all people have the equal right to pass political sovereignty onto their offspring. In this manner, everyone in a republic is equal to kings and queens in nonrepublics.

In contrast, in nonrepublics such as kingships and social democracies, people are born subject to an artificial political sovereign. This can only be achieved unnaturally – and thus criminally – through force or fraud by the political sovereign.

Force is asserted under the principle of might makes right. Fraud is achieved when the political sovereign misrepresents itself as having authority – often God-given authority – to define other people's rights and morality.

However, natural law defines what is moral and immoral in a republic. It defines political power to be equal. It defines force, theft and fraud as criminal. This is because force, theft and fraud violate the Golden Rule and are predatory.

In a republic, which adheres to natural political law, anyone acting like a king – usurping others' rights by force, theft or fraud – is to be treated as a tort feasor. Because all natural persons in republics have a natural law duty to refrain from violating other people's political rights, then all natural persons must refrain from using force, theft or fraud to achieve their goals or status. That is, all natural persons must refrain from acting like predators or kings to achieve their wishes.

Involuntary transactions are violations of natural law because they are predatory and are based on unequal power. Natural political law dictates that transactions be honest and consensual so that we treat each other equally and adhere to the Golden Rule.

Thus, natural political law precludes all natural persons from predatory behavior to accomplish their goals. Natural law prohibits murder, stealing, and defrauding (cheating) others for any reason.

It also prescribes punishment, including enslavement, for the commission of such crimes, which are facts of nature. In the republican form of government of the United States, torts and crimes are scientifically provable as natural facts by objective and verifiable evidence of injury and causation.

If citizens have no natural authority to use force, theft or fraud to achieve their goals, then citizens cannot delegate such power to their government. Thus in republics, which derive their moral authority from their citizens, there is no moral authority for government to use force, theft or fraud to achieve any of its citizens' unnatural wishes. This means that citizens' republican governments do not have authority to act like kings, which power exceeds nature's equal standards.

A government that usurps people's natural reserved power and which imposes unnatural duties upon natural persons is a government of the nonrepublican form. Under the political laws of nature, whose Golden Rule defines right and wrong, then such an unnatural, fraudulent and forceful government is either tortious or criminal, depending on the degree of harm.

Such a nonrepublican government adheres to the law of the jungle instead of the rule of (natural) law. Such a government fraudulently defines law as not answerable to nature, and uses force and deceit to achieve its goals.

This behavior is *per se* nonrepublican because it cannot stem from the natural delegated power of republican citizens. For example, republican citizens have no natural authority to take other people's personal property or to enslave others for their property use. Thus, they cannot delegate such authority to their republican governments, and such governments do not legitimately have such power.

Therefore, putting people in jail for certain property possession and for disfavored commerce is *per se* nonrepublican. Such power does not derive from the natural and moral criminal authority of the people, individual or combined. [70]

If we add up each of citizens' individual authority to enslave others for their nonviolent property use, which sum would equal zero, then the government representing citizens' moral authority would also have zero authority to enslave people for their property. "No law has any effect, of its own force, beyond the limits of the sovereignty from which its authority is derived," poignantly wrote the U.S. Supreme Court in *Hilton v. Guyot* (1895). [71]

Citizens may not delegate moral authority to republican governments to use force, theft or fraud to achieve their happiness because they do not naturally have such moral power to delegate. Instead, the opposite is true. They owe a natural duty to not initiate force or fraud against others at all times.

This adherence to the Golden Rule is to prevent not only citizens but also their government agents from preying upon weaker people. In fact, it requires obedience by government officials to the interests of fellow citizens. It objectively defines both morality and moral government.

As agents of the people, public servants have no authority to initiate force, theft or fraud to achieve anyone's political goals. Instead, in a republic, to act in such a way is criminal.

Likewise, because crime in a republic is defined by natural law, and not by Man, then republican legislatures may not grant their government agents with the authority to commit torts or crimes. Because in a republic, natural criminal standards apply to everyone equally, then republican legislatures may not exempt their agents from criminal prosecution, as a king can his.

In an American republic, all people are created equal to kings and queens. As well, all hopeful kings are subject to the political laws of nature, which means equality before the law.

In contrast, in nonrepublics the political sovereign usurps other people's natural power, claiming the unnatural or supernatural authority 1) to define other people's rights, and 2) to use force, theft or fraud, i.e., to commit crime, to achieve the sovereign's political will.

The fraud is to claim that people are born subject to a king or legislature's law. Because this nonrepublican principle violates the Golden Rule, and its natural political equality, then such form is *per se* immoral, or opposed to natural morality.

Because the political sovereign defines rights and duties in nonrepublics, then the sovereign's subjective standards define criminal justice instead of nature's objective ones, based on injury. Because nonrepublics use force, theft and fraud to achieve their political goals, then they are – by definition – naturally tortious or criminal.

This is because there is no natural law check upon their predatory, positive law authority. They can and do deprive people of their liberty based on artificial and subjective criteria.

We have seen that nonrepublics result from claims of supernatural power of some people over others. Such nonrepublics are not based on the consent authority of the people, but instead on the principle that the might of the ruler makes moral right.

Ironically, in a nonrepublic, the sovereign uses force, theft and fraud, which are naturally immoral and criminal, to define what is criminal and what is immoral. All nonrepublics are based on such corruption.

In contrast, justice in republics stems from the delegation of natural moral authority by the people. This limits the criminal authority of a republic to be no greater than that of each individual. Likewise, each individual carries the criminal authority of the state to, under certain circumstances, prevent and defend against crime and to arrest criminals.

Generally speaking – and notwithstanding the right of self-defense – to assert power over other people is not a moral right within a republic, but is instead a natural tort or crime. Because of natural equality under republican law, would-be kings are not exempt from tort and criminal liability. For republican officials to act like kings – outside of their delegated authority – is to act unlawfully under false color of law.

Republics are secular governments

Hearkening back to our thematic outline on pages 26 – 30, the third main difference between republics and nonrepublics is how they function. Republics operate as secular governments where rights and justice are defined scientifically. In contrast, nonrepublics – even those without state-recognized religions – function essentially as religious governments where justice is based on unprovable beliefs and opinions.

That the United States republic is to operate as a secular, non-religious government is punctuated by the 1st Amendment to the U.S. Constitution. It says that "Congress shall make no law respecting the establishment of religion, or prohibiting the free exercise thereof..."

This amendment is in league with the Title of Nobility Clause at Article I, Section 9, Clause 8 of the U.S. Constitution, and with similar clauses in state constitutions, that prohibit American republics from granting Titles of Nobility. Both the 1st Amendment and the Titles of Nobility Clause were specifically intended to prevent the creation of a monarchical government based on religion and privileged status.

The Bill of Rights, including the 1st Amendment, was enacted to shore up any misunderstanding in the original republican U.S. Constitution. Thus, the 1st Amendment reiterated, was redundant of, and clarified what was already a fundamental element of the republican form of government – that the government is secular or non-religious.

This amendment, as with all ten of the Bill of Rights, reserves substantive rights that are intended to secure the natural rights of individuals. The above quotation from the 1st Amendment explicitly does two things: 1) it prevents a state religion, such as in a monarchy, and 2) it reserves for individuals' the right to exercise their chosen religion or right of conscience.

In other words, it secures the natural right of conscience from a religious government. However, as I also hope to show here, not just the 1st Amendment, but in fact all of the Bill of Rights serve to prevent rule by opinion and belief of all kinds – not just those that sustain churches, temples and synagogues.

The republican form of government is secular in that its justice toward natural persons is based on natural, objective and provable criteria. Republics are secular in that they require natural objective criteria to define such concepts as crime, natural law citizens, property, and production.

Although many monarchies throughout history have relied upon the support of a religion as a moral or political crutch, in truth all nonrepublics are religious in nature 1) because they are based on an unprovable belief or opinion that one person or group of people can dictate the political rights and wrongs of others, and 2) because they lack a judicial jurisdiction (or justice system) that uses natural and objective criteria to determine right from wrong.

One such belief is in the moral authority of the sole political sovereign who has asserted unnatural or supernatural power to define the rights of other people. Another such belief is in the wisdom of this political sovereign to provide justice based on its subjective criteria, rather than upon natural and objective standards, as justice is rendered in a republic.

That one man or a group of legislators have supernatural power to define others' rights and to define who belongs in jail is not objectively provable. This situation exists only by force, theft or fraud, which such means are naturally criminal.

The propositions that non-crimes are crimes, that naturalized citizens are natural born Citizens, and that one's natural rights are actually positive law rights that are subject to government are all unprovable. This makes them mere beliefs or opinions upon which scientific natural justice cannot exist.

Religion "in its broadest sense," writes *Black's Law Dictionary*, "includes all forms of <u>belief</u> in the existence of superior beings exercising power over human beings by volition..." [72] *Black's* defines a belief as "a conviction of the truth of a proposition, existing subjectively in the mind...arising not from actual perception or knowledge, but by way of inference..." [73]

Thus, by definition, religion is an unprovable and subjective belief.

In contrast, law is objective and provable. Law's science, called jurisprudence, is a science based upon natural, objective and verifiable criteria. Most religions are not.

As we previously showed, natural law defines right and wrong, as well as republics' criminal jurisdiction. This means that criminal justice is not subject to any belief or opinion, religious or otherwise. It is not subject to Man's subjectivity or to certain people's unprovable supernatural claims of power over other people.

As also noted, natural law defines America's primary citizens. All natural born Citizens can be proven by the D.N.A. of their U.S. citizen fathers. Thus, to equate natural born Citizens with naturalized ones is subjective, false and disprovable.

Traditionally, natural law has also defined the meaning of marriage in a republic. It is a union between a man and a woman. This was the definition of marriage under the common law and in the law jurisdiction. This natural law jurisdiction does not recognize or sanction same-sex marriages.

The institution of marriage predates all ancient and modern governments. Therefore it is not defined by inconsistent positive law that is written down by legislatures or courts. In republics, neither legislatures nor courts have delegated authority to redefine natural terms for natural persons in the law jurisdiction. As with the natural meaning of crime, republican governments did not create marriage, and they are not in charge of defining it.

While modern marriage serves many private objectives (for example, to get better insurance rates, tax rates, intestate rights, hospital visitation rights, and loans), marriage serves no other public function than to define the political rights of a couple's natural offspring. This is to say that republican law recognizes marriage as a natural political right between men and women solely to determine the political rights of children. Otherwise governments have no intrinsic or legitimate interests in how people run their private relationships.

Thus, if it was not for the natural offspring of heterosexual sex, then the recognition of marriage would not exist under any natural or positive law. If it was not for determining the rights of children, then heterosexual couples would order their affairs just like everyone else – that is, privately.

Given this background, it is essential to recognize that the vast majority of modern heterosexual marriages are not natural law marriages, but are instead positive law marriages. They are marriages under the equity jurisdiction, and not the law jurisdiction. They are unions not only created under license by the states, but they are normally officiated by religious organizations that also exist solely by government privilege.

These licensed marriages exist not only to determine the rights of couples' offspring, but to involve the equity jurisdiction of the states when the unions break up. Couples voluntarily consent to have their unions governed under equity for the perceived benefits that licensed marriage offers.

Which brings us to the topic of same-sex marriages. Although such marriages are not recognized under natural law, i.e., there are no common law same-sex marriages, nothing is constitutionally stopping legislatures from granting same-sex couples the privilege of equitable, positive law marriage just as they do to heterosexual couples. In fact, the Equal Protection clause of the 14th Amendment likely demands it.

Natural law defines not only marriage, but also property. Property is anything to which the concept of ownership can attach. The Supreme Court in *Yick Wo v. Hopkins* (1886) wrote that one's rights to life, liberty, property, and the pursuit of happiness are "considered as indivi-dual possessions." [74] Ownership secures the exclusive use and enjoyment of things, including one's body and one's intangible rights.

One's body and one's rights are one's property because they do not belong to anyone else. This is a self-evident fact of natural reality. One's lawfully acquired property and other rights are facts of nature, which are provable.

Republican legislatures may not trespass upon one's property rights without compensation. Nor may they uphold people's natural right to acquire, possess and defend some property, while punishing the possession and use of other property.

Thus in America's republics, as long as such things as crime, citizenship, marriage and property are based on natural law, are defined naturally and logically, and are not subject to the beliefs and opinions of legislators, then religion does not and cannot define the government's treatment of individuals. Justice serves natural law, such as the laws of compensation and equality, and not any unnatural rights and duties that are imposed by legislatures, which are based on subjectivity and unprovable claims of legitimacy.

The legitimacy of any branch of republican government to violate one's natural rights to life, liberty, religion and property is unprovable, at least for example in my home state Indiana. That is, constitutional, statutory and case law in

Indiana support people's natural rights to acquire and possess any property, including for instance disfavored drugs.

Article I, Section 1 of the Indiana Constitution (1816) recognizes the natural, inherent and unalienable right to acquire, possess and defend property. This right was recognized by the Indiana Supreme Court in *Beebe v. State of Indiana* (1855) which declared as unconstitutional state legislation that criminally prohibited alcohol possession.

The Court wrote that "the express provisions of the constitution secure to the citizen his property and its reasonable use, (and) the legislature can not take away the right by any legerdemain of legislation." [75]

Equally, Indiana's statutory law also recognizes individuals' natural right to acquire and possess drugs. At IC 35-48-3-3 the Indiana Code exempts drug users from registering with the state's drug regulators, and says that these users may "lawfully possess" drugs for their own use.

Likewise, the Indiana Code does not criminally prohibit drug possession or dealing. At IC 35-48-4 *et seq.* the legislature merely calls this behavior a felony or misdemeanor.

However, merely calling any behavior a crime, such as standing on one's head, does not make it so. This is because the words case, controversy, misdemeanor, felony, crime, criminal case, and offense have inherent meanings under the U.S. and state constitutions, and do not answer to any legislature.

Within America's republics, each and all of these constitutional terms refer to injurious *malum in se* behavior. Each term refers to an injurious natural fact.

This injury requirement establishes judicial subject matter jurisdiction which is objective. "The requirement of injury in fact is a hard floor of Article III [judicial] jurisdiction that cannot be removed by statute," wrote the U.S. Supreme Court in *Summers v. Earth Island Institute* (2009). [76]

Thus, the idea that republican statutes criminally outlaw certain drugs, or certain property, is sheer fanciful opinion. It is an opinion or belief 1) because it is not provable, 2) because it is subjective (not based on objective positive law as cited above) and 3) because it presumes supernatural powers not granted to the Indiana legislature, e.g., a) the power to criminally prohibit anything, b) the power to change the criminal subject matter jurisdiction of judicial courts, and c) the power to put disfavored non-criminals in jail, in violation of the 13th Amendment.

As we already learned, what is criminally prohibited is naturally prohibited. The Indiana legislature was not granted power to redefine the meaning of crime, to change the criminal jurisdiction of Indiana's judicial courts, or to usurp the role of nature in criminal law. To think otherwise is not provable.

The role of legislatures in criminal law is to codify crimes and apportion punishment based on the severity of harm. But it takes a constitutional amendment – and not mere legislation – to change the criminal power of the judicial branch, which the legislature did not create. Thus, that Indiana's legislators have superior authority to define other people's rights is an unnatural, unobjective and unprovable opinion.

As mentioned above, the 1st Amendment in part prohibits the U.S. government from imposing religion or interfering in one's religion. It secures natural persons' natural right of conscience by depriving legislatures of the power to religiously, unnaturally and unscientifically define crime.

As we shall see, individuals' natural right of liberty is secured in the law jurisdiction of the judicial branch. The role of the law jurisdiction and its scientific approach is to exclude government from using religion or other beliefs and opinions in its treatment of natural persons.

However, this does not preclude the legislative and executive branches, called the political branches, from relying on religion or other unprovable beliefs and opinions in the operation of their equity jurisdiction. These branches are not precluded from treating their artificial creations subjectively, unscientifically and based on an opinion or even religion.

This is 1) because the 1st Amendment does not apply to artificial persons, and 2) because artificial persons are creations of the political sovereign – with only the privileges, powers and attributes granted by the sovereign. As we will discuss later, part one of the prior sentence conflicts with Supreme Court opinions in *First National Bank of Boston v. Bellotti* (1978) and *Citizens United v. Federal Election Commission* (2010). [77]

An example of the political branches being unscientific and opinionated is the scheduling of cannabis as a Class I controlled substance by the Drug Enforcement Administration. A Class I drug is one legislated to be without medicinal value.

However, as the medical cannabis movement and industry attest, both the CBD and THC cannabinoids in cannabis have enormous healing power under a variety of circumstances. These cannabinoids help make cannabis the most healthful plant on Earth.

Yet, as late as August 2016, the D.E.A. reaffirmed its opinionated, unscientific and completely illogical dogma that cannabis has no medicinal value. This is the same degree of dogmatic arbitrariness and denial of objective process that astronomer Galileo Galilei perhaps faced when explaining his theory of the solar system to his religious inquisitors.

However, because individuals in republics are not naturally subject to an artificial political sovereign, as was Galileo, and may or may not consent to its jurisdiction, which was compulsory upon him, then it is their choice to consent to its subjectivity, arbitrariness and artificial power over them.

Until they do, then they are to operate in a natural and objective judicial jurisdiction, where right, wrong and truth are based on natural and objective criteria, and not on the will of an artificial sovereign.

For example, until natural persons enter the government's artificial jurisdiction over drug commerce, such as by selling cannabis in state licensed dispensaries, then they are not subject to the D.E.A.'s ridiculous beliefs and opinions. How the

D.E.A. classifies cannabis has no direct effect on individuals' natural right to lawfully acquire it from any seller, or to lawfully grow (produce) it for themselves within America's republics.

One's rights to cannabis in the law jurisdiction do not depend on what positive law authorities say about it. Government's unprovable opinions and beliefs in their positive law do not change natural right and wrong, do not apply to natural persons, and do not change their natural rights.

However, all commercial growers and sellers of cannabis are subject to the D.E.A.'s beliefs and opinions. This is because all such commercial enterprises have consented to the agency's regulatory power over drug commerce.

Because artificial rights are bestowed rights, then artificial persons have no religious or free speech rights unless their sovereign grants these "rights" to them. And if artificial persons are given these political privileges, then they are not natural political rights that are unalienable and secured to individuals by the Bill of Rights, but instead are artificial regulated ones, subject to whims of the legislative sovereign.

In its artificial jurisdiction over its artificial creations, the legislative sovereign (and its agents) can define medicine not to be medicine. These of course are opinions, but they operate only in the positive law jurisdiction where the political sovereign defines artificial persons' artificial reality.

However, legislative or regulative positive law has no authority to define or redefine nature for natural persons. Legislatures cannot redefine natural reality, including natural political law. As we shall shortly see, this is because positive law and natural law are enforced in separate judicial jurisdictions, called equity and law.

Law is the judicial jurisdiction that adjudicates the natural rights of natural persons, based on objective science. Equity is the political sovereign's jurisdiction over artificial persons.

The sovereign over law is nature. Its adjudications are based on science. Its standards are immutable.

70

The sovereign over equity is the political sovereign. Its adjudications are based on belief and opinion, which can be arbitrary and capricious.

Because natural persons are not subject to equity, and because they operate in a separate judicial jurisdiction, then they are not subject to a legislative sovereigns' subjective and whimsical beliefs and opinions, as are artificial persons.

Republics keep powers separate

Many readers are familiar with the constitutional doctrine regarding the separation of republican powers. It is called the Separation of Powers Doctrine. It refers to provisions in most state constitutions which say that the powers and functions of each of the three branches of republican government shall be kept separate. The Indiana Constitution reads:

"The powers of the Government of Indiana shall be divided into three distinct departments, and each of them be confided to a separate body of Magistracy, to wit: those which are Legislative to one, those which are Executive to another, and those which are Judiciary to another: And no person or collection of persons, being of one of those departments, shall exercise any power properly attached to either of the others, except in the instances herein expressly permitted." [78]

This example of the separation of powers, i.e., that between the branches of republican governments, shall be discussed in particular later. But far from being unique, it is only one of the various separations of power that are necessary to sustain the republican form of government and federalism within the United States.

As we shall more thoroughly discuss, this Separation of Power Doctrine is active not only:

- between the legislative, executive and judicial branches of government, but also
- between the powers of America's sovereign positive law governments and the reserved natural law jurisdiction of individual sovereigns,
- between the powers of America's territorial sovereigns,
- between republics' two judicial jurisdictions, i.e., law and equity,
- between republics' two police powers, i.e., criminal prohibition and regulation,
- between Congress' legislative jurisdiction and that of the states,
- between Congress legislating with regard to the states and Congress legislating with regard to the federal areas, and
- between the police powers operating in the federal areas and those operating within the states.

Each of these separations of power are individually discussed in the remainder of this book. In order to understand America's republican statutes properly, readers must be aware of each of these separations of power. Otherwise, readers are incapable of understanding statutory law and of upholding America's republican form of government and federalism.

Students who graduate from American law schools cannot know law, which the Supreme Court says is the definition and limitation of power, without knowing how republican constitutions distribute power in the above ways. To know the above separations of power is to know American law. Most everything else is belief and opinion.

In contrast to republics, there really is no constitutional Separation of Powers Doctrine that operates in nonrepublics, such as in monarchies. This is because in nonrepublics, all government departments, all the powers of government and all the rights of people are creations of and serve the legislative sovereign, be it a parliament or a king. This sovereign can distribute power as it sees fit, unless it has agreed not to.

In such a nonrepublic, all power resides in a sole sovereign, and everyone and everything is subject to this power. The political sovereign is the sole source of law in a nonrepublic. People look to it for their political rights.

In contrast, in republics, organic citizens' political rights are naturally inherited, and such rights are not defined by government. Instead, government serves to secure these rights.

The separation of power by territory

The first and most obvious separation of powers within the United States is that between the state republics. The states have separate sovereignty over their own land areas. The "jurisdiction of a state is co-extensive with its territory; co-extensive with its legislative power..." summarized the court reporter in *Bevans v. United States* (1818). [79]

For example, the Ohio legislature does not regulate gun dealing in Pennsylvania, but only in Ohio. As well, Pennsylvania's courts do not adjudicate crimes that occur in New Jersey.

Each state has its own territorial jurisdiction, and the extent of state power is territorial. For example, Wyoming's motor vehicle statutes do not apply in Alabama.

Given as a general rule that sovereignty is territorial, Congress as a legislature also has its own territory over which it legislates. These areas are called the federal areas. They are different than and separate from the land area making up the fifty states over which, according to the U.S. Constitution, Congress must legislate as a republic.

Thus, Congress legislates as a republic over the subject matter that the U.S. Constitution grants it power within the republican states. As well, it legislates as does a sovereign state over the activities that occur within the federal areas.

This means that Congress has exclusive jurisdiction over certain territory as do the states. This also means that Congress legislates in two capacities: 1) as a republic with regard to the fifty states, and 2) in a municipal or local capacity with regard to the federal areas, including over the nation's coastal and navigable waterways.

The U.S. Constitution at Article I, Section 8, Clause 17 grants Congress legislative jurisdiction over the ten square miles of the District of Columbia and over enclaves within the states "purchased by the Consent of the Legislature of the State... for the Erection of Forts, Magazines, Arsenals, dock-Yards and other needful Buildings."

These federal areas are defined in the United States Code at 18 USC 7. These areas include 1) the District of Columbia; 2) the federal territories (Guam, Puerto Rico, Marianas Islands, American Samoa and the Virgin Islands); 3) the above-mentioned U.S. enclaves within the states; 4) America's coastline and navigable waterways; 5) all ships, airplanes and spaceships registered to the U.S., and 6) anywhere in the world (outside of the U.S.) where a crime is committed against a Citizen of the United States.

For example, a murder of an American in Benghazi, Libya is subject to U.S. criminal law. That is why the F.B.I. traveled there to investigate the murders of four Americans on September 11, 2012. Murders in Washington, D.C. are also subject to U.S. law. However, murders that occur in Virginia, for example, are Virginian crimes, subject to Virginia's law authorities.

As well, because Congress is sovereign over navigable waterways within the United States, and over ships and airplanes registered to the U.S., then it – and not the states – is sovereign over the adjudication of crime on such U.S. waterways, ships and airplanes. [80] Notwithstanding statutory exceptions, anyone on an American airplane or ship is subject to the same U.S. criminal law as if they were in Washington, D.C.

This is an example of the separation of sovereignty be-

74

tween the territorial jurisdictions of the states and the jurisdiction of Congress over everything else. This "everything else" includes 1) U.S. land areas outside of the states, 2) U.S. enclaves within the states, 3) U.S. navigable waters outside of, within and between the states; and 4) the ships, spaceships and airplanes registered to the U.S. In these places, U.S. criminal law applies.

This shows that there is a political sovereign over every single cubic inch of the rivers, land and air within the United States. Again, the role of law is to define which sovereign has power over what, and what the scope of this power is.

Therefore, within the country named the United States there are both 1) fifty-one (51) territorial sovereigns, each and all with their own civil and criminal powers over that which occurs within their land, air or water areas, and 2) one blanket national sovereign, i.e., Congress as the U.S. republic, that legislates as a republic over certain subject matter within the land areas of the states, which are outside of the federal areas. More on this later.

The separation of natural and positive law

As we have seen since the beginning of this book, the republican form of government is one that recognizes the dual sovereignty of nature and Man, or natural law and Man's positive law. Nature's political jurisdiction is over natural persons and their natural duties. These individuals naturally adjudicate all their own decisions within their own sovereignty, unless they invoke the judicial law jurisdiction by harming others.

In contrast, Man's legislative positive law jurisdiction is largely over commerce, immigration and governmental affairs. Man's legislative jurisdiction does not define the rights of natural persons or of natural law citizens. This positive law jurisdiction applies only to artificial persons, including artificial, adopted 14th Amendment citizens.

Without prior mention of the Separation of Powers Doctrine, we observed several examples of how positive and natural law are kept separate in republics. We first observed how differently Congress treats the offspring of unwed U.S. fathers from the offspring of unwed U.S. mothers in foreign countries. This difference in statutory treatment at 8 USC 1409 (a) and (c) is due to the recognition of the dual sovereignty of natural and positive law as applied to these offspring.

Thus this separation between the natural law jurisdiction and positive law jurisdiction plays out in U.S. citizenship statutes. This means that Americans must know about this duality in order to understand citizenship and their citizenship rights.

Under natural political law, the rights of citizenship follow the father, regardless where his children are born. (That is one reason why Article II, Section 1, Clause 5 of the U.S. Constitution has a 14-year residency requirement, but no born-in-America mandate to be President.)

Because of the natural fact that no one is a witness to the fatherhood of a child, natural law requires the father to claim the child into the political society. As we have seen, this is accomplished through marriage to the mother or by oath.

Thus, the positive law jurisdiction of Congress looks to the natural law jurisdiction of the U.S. father to secure natural law citizenship for his children. This shows that the U.S. father's power to make natural citizens is antecedent, superior to and preeminent to the power of Congress to make naturalized citizens, such that even Congress defers to U.S. fathers' natural political authority.

And in the absence of a citizen father, or when a citizen father's political authority to claim his child lapses, the 14th Amendment and Congress look to adopt the child as a Citizen of the United States. [81] This is based on the mother's U.S. nationality or on the child's birth on U.S. soil. [82]

A second interesting example of the separation of natural and positive law regards the natural right of self-defense. Because each natural person in a republic has natural rights to life and property, then each person has a natural right to defend this life and property. This is the right to use sufficient force to defend one's person or property, or that of another.

What is illustrative for our purposes is that the natural right of self-defense is actually America's primary criminal jurisdiction. For example, suppose Person A pulls a gun on Person B with the apparent intent to kill him.

Person A is committing a crime because he does not have a natural right (or legal privilege) to harm or threaten others. Such violence violates the natural right of Person B to not be harmed or threatened. Thus, Person B has the natural right to use sufficient force, for example his own gun, to prevent being harmed.

This is a natural right in a republic. Such right comes from nature, and does not derive from one's legislature. No one naturally looks to a legislature for the right to defend themselves, particularly in the heat of a violent moment.

"(T)he execution of the law of nature is, in that state, put into every man's hands, whereby every one has a right to punish the transgressors of that law to such a degree, as may hinder its violation," wrote Locke. [83]

If Person B exercises this natural right of self-defense properly, then the criminal law jurisdiction of government is secondary, and is thus not invoked. This is because the natural law jurisdiction of prospective crime victims is the primary jurisdiction where crime can first be adjudicated.

Only if Person B gets injured or adjudicates the matter wrongly is the natural criminal law jurisdiction of the government (over injury to natural persons) appealed to. The right of self-defense is proof that individuals, and not republican governments, have primary subject matter jurisdiction over crime when faced with the prospect of being a criminal victim.

A third example of the separation of natural from positive law is discernible from the statutory distinction between production and manufacturing. In republics, individuals have jurisdiction over what they produce for themselves and their households, whereas the positive law has authority over what people produce for distribution to others, called commerce.

This distinction is seen respectively in the Indiana Controlled Substances Act at IC 35-48-1-18 and -26 and in the U.S. Controlled Substances Act at 21 USC 802(15) and (22), where manufacturing is contrasted with production.

Growing, for instance, tomatoes or cannabis for oneself and one's household is treated by republics differently than growing tomatoes or cannabis for others. Republics are granted authority to regulate the commerce in tomatoes and cannabis, but not one's self-production. As we shall see, legislative prohibitions (called *malum prohibita*) do not operate in the natural jurisdiction of individuals, but apply only to regulated commercial behavior that is disfavored by legislatures. [84]

A fourth example of the separation of the natural law jurisdiction of the individual from the positive law of the political sovereign is also from America's Controlled Substances Acts, all of which respect the natural right of drug possession within America's republics. Because these statutes are written to be consistent with U.S. and state constitutions, then the statutes support, for example, the natural right to acquire, possess, use, share and defend personal property, such as disfavored drugs.

This is evident from Indiana's IC 35-48-3-3(e), as defined at IC 35-48-1-27, and in the U.S. Controlled Substances Act at 21 USC 822(c), as defined by 21 USC 802(27). These statutes say that drug users may "lawfully possess" controlled substances for their own use and the use of their households. The natural right to "lawfully possess" property includes the natural right to lawfully acquire and produce property for oneself, noted above.

To lawfully acquire anything is to acquire it without use of force, theft or fraud. This includes acquiring property consensually from any purveyor, and producing (or growing) such property for oneself.

Purveyors of goods and services are subject to regulation,

78

but consumers or self-producers who operate in the natural law jurisdiction are not. Consumers may lawfully acquire any property from any person 1) who lawfully holds such property and 2) who is willing to sell or trade it to them.

If consumers or self-producers were subject to positive law instead of to their own whims and budgets, then legislatures could tell them what to grow or what to purchase, just as legislatures tell merchants what they may do.

That republican legislatures do not tell consumers what to purchase is an admission that consumers operate in a jurisdiction that is unassailable by legislatures. Individuals have a natural right to consume. Merchants of goods and services are regulated, but ordinary consumers and self-producers – who are operating under natural law – are not.

(Note that Obamacare's personal mandate to purchase health insurance is not an exception to the above rule. Obamacare does not impose a duty upon natural persons to purchase insurance. For example, babies were not required to buy it. Instead, Obamacare imposes an artificial duty upon artificial persons, called U.S. individual income taxpayers, who have already consented to be governed by the income tax system.)

This means that Congress can tell its artificial creations, such as income taxpayers, what they must do with their dollars. However, it has no authority over those natural persons and natural law citizens who live off the land, who do not earn income, and who have not entered Congress' taxing system.

Thus, just as Congress looks first to the authority of U.S. citizen fathers 1) to secure the natural inherited political rights of their offspring, republican judicial courts look first to the natural jurisdiction of individuals 2) to defend themselves from crime, 3) to produce things for themselves, and 4) to lawfully acquire and possess property.

The above sentence highlights four examples that republican law, which is the definition of power in an American republic, apportions this power between the positive law authority of government and the reserved natural law authority of individuals.

This distinction between the positive and natural law jurisdictions is the primary separation of powers discernible in American republican law. The existence of the natural law jurisdiction is self-evident from the reservation of natural rights expressed in state constitutions and in the 9th and 10th Amendments to the U.S. Constitution.

The recognition of the natural law jurisdiction is the basis and cause-in-fact of America's republican form of government. Without the recognition of natural law, and without a separation of natural and positive law, there can be no republic.

The separation of law and equity

As there are two forms of law (natural law and positive law), then there are two separate judicial jurisdictions within America's republics – law and equity – to respectively deal with natural and positive law issues. Article III, Section 2 of the U.S. Constitution says that judicial power of the United States shall extend to cases and controversies in law and equity.

(Note that Article III also grants various other jurisdictions to the U.S. judicial branch. This includes jurisdiction over admiralty and maritime cases, which will be discussed later. Because all navigable U.S. waterways are defined to be in the federal areas, then states have no regulatory or criminal jurisdiction over such waterways.)

All republican judicial decisions are based upon matters of law or equity. They are made by courts either in the courts' original or appellate capacity. This means that judicial decisions come 1) from trial courts having original or subject matter jurisdiction over cases, or 2) from courts' appellate powers to review the propriety of lower judicial or administrative court decisions. [85]

As natural law applies to natural persons and positive law

80

applies to artificial persons, the law jurisdiction applies to natural persons and the equity jurisdiction applies to artificial persons. All persons can determine which judicial jurisdiction they are in by examining the nature of the rights that they seek to enforce or defend.

Injuries or violations to the natural rights of natural persons, called torts and crimes, are adjudicated in the law jurisdiction of the judicial branch. Injury or harm to the contractual or commercial rights of artificial persons are adjudicated in the equity jurisdiction of judicial courts.

In civil cases, but not criminal cases, these jurisdictions have been procedurally merged. This means that both civil cases in equity and civil cases at law use the same courts and same procedures. However, their procedures and remedies have not been merged in criminal cases because equity has no criminal jurisdiction.

"Equity is a body of jurisprudence, or field of jurisdiction, differing in its origin, theory, and methods from the common law;" writes *Black's Law Dictionary*, "though procedurally, in the federal courts and most state courts, equitable and legal rights and remedies are administered in the same court." [86] Part of the Founding Fathers' brilliance was to combine these two systems of justice into state and federal judicial courts.

These state and federal republican courts throughout the United States adjudicate cases in either law or equity based on the facts and parties of each case. Whether a case involves natural or artificial persons, involves natural duties or artificial duties, and involves natural or artificial rights will determine 1) whether law or equity has jurisdiction over the subject matter, and 2) whether the matter is subject to criminal law.

Because natural persons are the subject matter of natural law, violations to their natural rights are the subject matter of the law jurisdiction. Because artificial, legal persons are the objects of positive law, then artificial rights are the subject matter of equity.

81

This ultimately and conceptually means that nature and her laws are sovereign over the law jurisdiction of judicial courts. In contrast, the legislative branch of republican government is sovereign over positive law, which operates in equity and applies only to artificial persons.

Law is strictly adjudicated in the judicial branch and, absent a constitutional amendment, is open only to that which is *malum in se* (wrong by its nature of injury). Its standards for judicial cases, crimes, citizenship and marriage for instance are strictly natural. It dispenses justice based on jurisprudence, which is the natural science of law.

In contrast, equity is adjudicated in both the executive and judicial branches. On one hand, to maintain public health and safety standards, exeutive branch agencies dispense licenses (privileges) to artificial persons to engage the public in commerce. This regulatory process operates by administrative law.

By comparison, judicial courts in equity both adjudicate disputes between artificial persons, such as corporations, and serve as appellate courts for decisions by lower equity courts, such as administrative law courts. Such administrative courts do not judge what is right and wrong. Instead, they administer the will of the legislature.

The law jurisdiction enforces only natural duties, such as the duty to not harm others. Equity enforces contractual, regulatory and other commercial duties to which artificial persons have consented.

Law's remedies include monetary compensation and restitution for torts, as well as incarceration and fines for crimes. Equity's commercial remedies include forfeiture of property, specific performance and injunction.

As mentioned, the law jurisdiction is American republics' only criminal jurisdiction. The equity jurisdiction has no criminal authority. Instead, equitable orders are enforced through judicial courts' contempt authority.

For example, drug regulators can enjoin (order to stop)

disfavored drug dealers from drug dealing. These administrative orders can be enforced by judicial courts using their contempt powers. Violators of judicial orders, such as recalcitrant drug dealers, can be incarcerated for contempt of court.

This incarceration is not for the crime of drug dealing. The commerce of any property is not a crime in a republic and is instead a regulated activity. The incarceration is for violating a judicial order, which comes only after the drug dealer has been given administrative due process in the executive branch. Thus ultimately, disfavored merchants can go to jail in republics for their unapproved commercial activity, such as drug dealing, but this is not because their commercial activity is criminal.

Cases and crimes are defined in the law jurisdiction by natural law always to include injury. Consensually providing goods and services to others does not ever constitute a case or crime unless it injures someone.

Thus, consensual and non-injurious business activity is not subject to the criminal law jurisdiction in a republic. Instead, one's purveying of goods or services is subject to equity, which enforces regulation, but which has no criminal authority.

Natural persons become subject to the law jurisdiction by negligently or intentionally violating the natural rights of other people. Artificial persons become subject to equity when they engage the public in commerce by selling goods or services.

These artificial persons become subject to judicial courts 1) when they harm the rights of natural or artificial persons or 2) as mentioned above, when they reach a court in its appellate capacity.

Whereas the basis of equity is the positive law of a legislative sovereign, the basis of the law jurisdiction is natural law, which is outside and beyond such legislative authority.

Whereas the legislature proscribes what is not allowed (*malum prohibita*) in equity, nature proscribes what is bad (*malum in se*) at law. Thus, law – including criminal law – has no authority over *malum prohibita*, which instead operates solely by regulation in equity.

So, regulation operates in equity over artificial persons who have consented to this commercial jurisdiction. In contrast, tortious and criminal prohibitions operate mandatorily upon individuals at law. Torts and crimes are either natural prohibitions, i.e., *malum in* se, or they are prohibitions that have been placed into the law jurisdiction by a constitutional amendment, such as was distributing alcohol.

In equity, legislatures legislate all legal rights (which are artificial privileges) and duties. At law, legislatures merely prescribe (write down) or codify pre-existing natural rights and duties. This is because republican legislatures are sovereign over equity, but are not sovereign over law.

Instead, nature defines the law jurisdiction. The law jurisdiction is short for the natural law jurisdiction. It is nature personified in substance and procedure – scientific natural law and its Golden Rule made flesh.

The basis of the law jurisdiction is this: that in exchange for the reservation of the natural benefits of individual sovereignty, which is independent of and above the positive law of legislatures and other people, then nature requires that we compensate people who we harm. The natural law of compensation is the basis – indeed moral authority – of American tort and criminal law.

In other words, the basis of the law jurisdiction is individual liberty and self-responsibility. Individuals remain free and sovereign over the natural law jurisdiction of republican constitutions, including its criminal jurisdiction, unless they cannot be self-responsible and are unable to properly self-govern. They even have liberty to lawfully defend their own lives and property if they exercise this natural right prudently.

When their actions go beyond that which is allowed in the natural law jurisdiction, i.e., when they negligently or intentionally violate the equal natural rights of other people, then the law jurisdiction of judicial courts gains authority over this natural law jurisdiction in order to adjudicate the injuries that they have caused to other people and their interests.

Thus, a natural person becomes subject to a judicial court's (natural, civil and / or criminal) law jurisdiction only when he or she negligently or intentionally harms another person or his interests. The law jurisdiction is a republic's authority over injury caused by natural persons, which are torts and crimes that humans for millennium have naturally opposed.

As we saw in our discussion of the natural right of self-defense, individual sovereigns as potential victims exercise primary jurisdiction over crime. As with all natural rights, when people exercise this right of self-defense irresponsibly, then the authority of the law jurisdiction – and maybe the criminal law jurisdiction – is invoked.

In contrast, artificial persons such as corporations, which exist solely by privilege of a legislature's positive law, do not have natural rights that are subject to adjudication in the law jurisdiction. Artificial persons are not subject to criminal law.

They do not have natural rights to which the Bill of Rights applies. Instead, they have positive-law, legal rights (which are revocable privileges) that are subject to a legislature's equity jurisdiction within an American republic. This of course is a non-criminal jurisdiction because republican legislatures cannot legislate (create) crimes.

The law and equity jurisdictions of judicial trial courts are based respectively on individual and commercial injury. The equity jurisdiction is also exercised by regulatory administrative law courts in the executive branch. The decisions of these latter courts, which dole out commercial privileges, are subject to review or enforcement by judicial courts, acting in their appellate capacity.

Only one of these jurisdictions has primary authority over any given subject matter. And only the law jurisdiction in a republic has criminal authority, which is the rightful power to incarcerate a natural person for a crime.

Equity lacks criminal jurisdiction ostensibly because governments cannot enslave artificial persons, such as businesses. Instead, republican governments have equitable authority to shut down and enjoin such unwanted artificial persons.

In America's republics, criminal law adjudicates only violations of natural duties by natural persons, who can be physically placed in jail. It does not adjudicate any duties imposed by positive law or by contract upon artificial persons and enterprises, which cannot be placed in jail. Ultimately, one cannot contract oneself into slavery or jail because modern contracts are subject to non-criminal equity.

Republican legislatures can legislate over commerce in equity, but 1) may not legislate over the duties of natural persons, and 2) may only prescribe (write down) and codify *malum in se* crimes that are already proscribed (prohibited) by nature and enforced in the law jurisdiction.

This translates into two important concepts: 1) that republican legislatures have no authority to write down crimes inconsistently with the natural and constitutional law definition of crime involving injury, and 2) that no commercial activity (except human slavery and trafficking) is subject to criminal law and criminal sanction within an American republic.

This means that states have no authority to treat any kind of commercial activity, such as prostitution or drug dealing, as criminal. This is because business activity is instead subject to regulation in their non-criminal equity jurisdiction. In other words, voluntary commerce – even unwanted commerce – cannot be criminal in a republic because it operates under regulation, which has no criminal power.

Consequently, statutes that define the equity jurisdiction in America's republics, such as states' administrative procedures acts, neither have criminal provisions in them nor have any criminal force or effect. Natural persons are only criminally subject to the law jurisdiction, where violations of natural rights and duties are adjudicated.

Statutes that define how a state is to regulate drug and gun commerce, for example, apply only to artificial, commercial persons, and do not apply to natural persons who merely possess drugs and guns. Personal use of any property is not commercial, and is thus not subject to regulation. Conversely, equity exists to adjudicate the privileges granted by kings and legislatures to artificial entities that have no natural rights.

Therefore, all the artificial privileges that republican legislatures bestow upon artificial persons operate under equity and have no recognition under the law jurisdiction – and thus, under the criminal law jurisdiction. The law jurisdiction serves only to adjudicate injury by natural persons, which is inherently wrong or *malum in se*.

This means that the law jurisdiction does not serve to adjudicate violations by artificial persons of political *malum prohibita*, which is commercial conduct that is disallowed – not by nature – but strictly by virtue of a statute or regulation in equity.

Some examples of *malum prohibita* include: 1) driving a car at a speed that exceeds a posted limit, 2) paying or receiving money for sex, 3) selling drugs, alcohol or guns without a license, 4) misapplying a tax deduction on an income tax form, 5) performing a professional service without a license, 6) deriving income from commercial gambling, and 7) not filing an income tax form when required.

These publicly disfavored activities are banned – not by the political laws of nature and its criminal law jurisdiction – but only by a legislature or regulatory agency, based on their beliefs and opinions.

Posted speed limits are based on the opinions of traffic safety specialists. Prostitutes are jailed based on the unprovable view that paying or receiving money for any service is a crime.

The war on drugs is based upon the opinions 1) that republican legislatures can ban personal property possession without a constitutional amendment, and 2) that certain manufacturers and distributors of drugs, e.g., pharmaceutical companies, are less criminal than others, e.g, corner drug dealers.

The licensing of professionals is based on beliefs and opinions about the quality of their professional training. The deductibility of an item on a tax form may be based on the licensure of such a professional.

These beliefs and opinions – operating upon artificial persons in equity – have nothing to do with right and wrong or true and false, as defined by nature, as applicable to natural persons, and as adjudicated at law in the law jurisdiction. Thus, these *malum prohibita* are not enforceable as torts or crimes in the law jurisdiction. They are enforceable only as regulatory violations upon artificial persons in equity, which is a non-criminal jurisdiction.

Accordingly, all criminal authority in America's republics is over natural persons in the law jurisdiction, which is not subject to statutes (or legislative belief and opinion) that are inconsistent with natural law and natural rights. This is in synch with the pillars of Justinian justice referred to by Blackstone, which "reduced the whole doctrine of law" to three principles: "that we should live honestly, should hurt nobody, and should render to every one his due." [87]

As we shall see, these precepts are the foundations for state and U.S. judicial courts. They are a succinct summary of law courts' subject matter jurisdiction over individuals. They also demonstrate how American law fulfills the Golden Rule of natural law, which defines right and wrong.

Statutes that define *malum prohibita* in equity do not define right and wrong, and thus do not define the natural duties of natural persons. This is because a legislature's equity jurisdiction does not apply to natural persons and cannot create duties in them.

This is consistent with the concept that legislatures' positive law jurisdiction does not apply in, and cannot inconsistently invade, the natural law jurisdiction of individuals or the law jurisdiction of judicial courts, where natural law is enforced.

Nor can positive law grant artificial privileges to natural persons. An example of an artificial privilege is that of "unlimited life" that states bestow upon corporations. Corporations are made to outlive their shareholders.

If republican legislatures had jurisdiction over natural persons – that is, if they could legislate over natural persons as they can over artificial persons – then they could bestow natural persons with unlimited life as they do corporations.

But of course legislatures cannot grant unlimited life to natural persons. They cannot legislate over nature. For example, they cannot legislate inconsistently with our natural law duties, such as our duties to not harm others.

Likewise, republican legislatures may not legislate inconsistently with how nature defines crime, marriage, lawful property possession, production and natural citizenship, which are subject to the law jurisdiction. This subject matter is beyond the authority of republican legislatures and judicial courts – just as is granting unlimited life to natural persons.

The law and equity sides of due process

Despite these differences between law and equity, the 14th Amendment makes clear that the principles of due process and equal protection apply to all persons, both natural and artificial. The amendment is principally about artificial citizens. It says that no state shall abridge the privileges and immunities of Citizens of the United States, who are adopted U.S. citizens.

However, the amendment also requires states to provide due process and equal protection to both natural and artificial persons. It reads: "nor shall any State deprive any person of life, liberty and property, without due process of law; nor to deny to any person within its jurisdiction the equal protection of the laws."

"Any person" means all natural and artificial persons, not

just artificial citizens, called Citizens of the United States, who exercise privileges and immunities. Because the rights of natural and artificial persons are adjudicated respectively in the law and equity jurisdictions, then versions of due process and equal protections are owed in each jurisdiction. These rights of natural and artificial persons are similar and analogous, but respectively different.

The due process of law that is required for natural persons is defined by the U.S. and state constitutions. In particular, the Bill of Rights (Amendments 1 – 10) are a rich source of these substantive rights, upon which natural rights depend.

These rights include, for example, the right to protection against unreasonable searches and seizures, the right to a presentment or indictment, the right against excessive bail, and the right to a jury trial in criminal matters. Such due process of law requires allegations of a civil or criminal case, i.e., based on an injury to a right, in order to invoke a judicial court's jurisdiction.

Artificial persons do not have these rights. The Bill of Rights does not apply to them. It does not apply in equity.

For example, artificial persons do not have the right to a jury trial in criminal matters. This is because artificial persons operate in equity and are not subject to the criminal law jurisdiction. Plus, equity has no criminal authority.

Because artificial persons are creations of republican legislatures, and because they consent to be governed by the rules laid down by legislatures, then the process by which government treats these artificial persons is defined by legislative statutes, instead of by constitutions. The 14th Amendment says that these statutes must provide due process.

This statutory process in equity is called administrative due process. It applies to anyone who owes artificial duties to government, such as taxes, or the duty to be registered as a business, or the duty to possess a drivers license.

This process is carried out in equity in the executive branch of government, and is enforced by the judicial branch in its appellate capacity. This administrative law process is generally described by state and U.S. administrative procedures acts.

So, artificial persons' due process operates under equity and is called administrative due process. These are the positive law procedures that legislatures define to assess and collect taxes, enforce ordinances, and to dispense or deny commercial privileges, for example.

Such commercial privileges include, for instance, building permits, professional licenses and drivers' licenses. All of these permissions operate under equity, subject to regulation in the executive branch of a republic. Adverse regulatory decisions are appealable to judicial courts.

This administrative process is analogous to due process of law in the judicial branch for natural persons. In most states administrative process includes, for example, the right to notice of a hearing or an order, the right to default or summary judgment, the right to have a representative, the right to an appealable order and the right to appeal an order. [88]

Administrative due process applies to artificial persons and is subject to the powers and remedies of equity, not law. Republics' equitable administrative remedies against unwanted businesses include investigation, confiscation and injunction. Once these statutory processes are exhausted in the executive branch, then judicial courts may proceed with forfeiture proceedings and judicial injunctions against regulatory violators.

Administrative due process is subject to the principle of exhaustion of administrative remedies. Before a party to an administrative action may seek a remedy from a judicial court, such administrative process must be exhausted.

For example, if a person gets denied a building permit, then the administrative process which rendered such adverse decision is subject to appeal in a judicial court. However this artificial legal right becomes effective only after the affected party has exhausted all administrative processes and remedies.

In general, writes the Indiana Supreme Court, "where an

administrative remedy is available, such remedy must be pursued before the claimant is allowed access to the courts." [89]

Likewise, if regulators seek a judicial injunction against *malum prohibita*, such as an unwanted drug business, then they must exhaust their administrative remedies before seeking a judicial court's help with enforcement. For example, under the Uniform Controlled Substances Act, this correct process would include unsuccessfully imposing an administrative injunction upon the drug business before seeking a judicial one, the latter which can be enforced by a judicial court's contempt powers. [90]

Because such unwanted commercial activity is regulated in the executive branch, then it is not subject to criminal law in the judicial branch. For example, IC 35-48-3-3(a) and (b) of the Indiana Controlled Substances Act require all persons which manufacture, distribute or dispense drugs to register with regulators in the Indiana pharmacy board. Likewise, 21 USC 822(a) requires all drug dealers to register with the D.E.A.

These are legislative admissions that manufacturing and selling drugs are regulated under equity in the executive branch, and are not subject to criminal law in the judicial branch. This is due to republican constitutions' Separation of Powers Doctrine, which we will discuss more thoroughly below.

The separation of law and equity is also demonstrated by how Congress treats natural law citizens (called natural born Citizens) and adopted positive law citizens (called Citizens of the United States) within America's republics. As we have seen, some naturalized citizens are creations of Congress, while natural born Citizens are creations of natural sexual congress.

As such, these natural law citizens owe Congress no positive law, legal duties. Such free citizens can consent to be governed by Congress only in the equity and admiralty jurisdictions where Congress rightly legislates over government affairs and commerce.

Ultimately Congress creates and may legislate over the political rights of Citizens of the United States, who are Congress' citizen-subjects. However Congress did not create and may not legislate over the inherited natural political rights of natural born Citizens, whose natural political rights do not come from and are antecedent to Congress.

This is because Citizens of the United States owe allegiance and duties to Congress that natural born Citizens do not. This is apparent from both 1) immigration and naturalization statutes and 2) draft registration statutes, as discussed below.

Natural born Citizens do not owe an allegiance to Congress that Citizens of the United States owe. This is apparent from 8 USC 1101(a)(22), which defines a national of the United States as "(A) a Citizen of the United States, or (B) a person who, though not a Citizen of the United States, owes permanent allegiance to the United States."

This statute clearly says that Citizens of the United States owe permanent allegiance to the United States, which means Congress. The issue for us is whether the term "national" includes natural born Citizens, such that they would also owe allegiance to Congress.

That natural born Citizens do not owe permanent allegiance to the United States under this statute is for several reasons. First, the term United States in the above-cited statute refers to a geographical territory, and not to the republican form of government to which natural law citizens would pledge their allegiance.

8 USC 1101(a)(38) defines the United States as "the continental United States, Alaska, Hawaii, Puerto Rico, Guam, the Virgin Islands of the United States, and the Commonwealth of the Northern Mariana Islands." Thus, the term United States is politically ambiguous because Congress does not owe Puerto Rico, Guam, the Virgin Islands and the Mariana Islands a republican form of government to which natural born Citizens would pledge allegiance.

Second, if the statute applied to natural born Citizens, then Congress could have directly said so. If the statute applied

93

to both kinds of U.S. citizens, then Congress could have used the same wording as it did at 8 USC 1409 (a) and (c) to refer to both kinds of U.S. citizens.

That is, it could have said that the statute applies to any person with "the nationality of the United States..." which description would have included natural born Citizens. That the statute did not read as such indicates Congress' intention to exclude natural born Citizens from the legislation's scope.

Third, as we have held all along, Congress does not legislate over natural born Citizens, who are exempt from its legislative jurisdiction. That is why 8 USC 1102(a)(22) does not refer to natural born Citizens, and why natural born Citizens owe their allegiance neither to Congress nor to the actual territory called the United States (as referred to in the statute). As *The Pledge of Allegiance* says, citizens owe their loyalties "to the republic" for which the U.S. flag stands. Citizens do not owe their loyalties to government or a branch such as Congress.

Fourth, a natural born Citizen is born free of Congress, and could never pledge "permanent allegiance" to the United States, which means Congress. This is because his or her right to be free is unalienable. Individual liberty may be deprived or indentured only as punishment for the commission of crime. As well, he or she always has the natural unalienable right to emigrate, which means to leave the country.

"Consult jurists, Grotius, Puffendorff, Burlamaqui, Vattel," wrote the U.S. Supreme Court in *Melvaine v. Coxe's Lessee* (1804), "They are of the opinion, that every man has a natural right to migrate, unless restrained by laws, and that these cannot restrain the right, but under special circumstances and in a limited degree." [91]

Thus, we can conclude that the definition of a "national" does not include a natural born Citizen, who owes no permanent allegiance to Congress. Congress treats Citizens of the United States and nationals differently than it does natural born Citizens. This is because only the former, who gain their political rights from Congress, owe Congress their allegiances.

In contrast, natural born Citizens who gain their citizenship apart from Congress, owe Congress no allegiance and duties. Instead, they owe to other people and citizens, called "We the People of the United States of America," natural political duties 1) to do others no harm, and 2) to come to their defense in event of wars, torts and crimes.

I mention torts and crimes in the above sentence not because people owe a natural law duty to defend other people from such unwanted behavior. Instead, I mention them because natural born Citizens owe a natural political duty to both 1) serve as jurors when summoned by a judicial court, and 2) to witness torts and crimes.

Because these terms are defined naturally, then individuals have a natural (perhaps codified) duty to report and witness *malum in se*. Natural political law duties are mandatory law duties. Competent U.S. citizens have a natural duty to witness, report and adjudicate (as jurors) natural wrongs occurring to their fellow natural persons. Naturally, this is how we would wish others to treat our rights.

That Congress treats naturalized Citizens of the United States differently than natural born Citizens is also apparent from draft registration statutes. 50 USC 3802(a) reads:

> "Except as otherwise provided in this chapter it shall be the duty of every male Citizen of the United States, and every other male person residing in the United States, who, on the day or days fixed for the first or any subsequent registration, is between the ages of eighteen and twenty-six, to present himself for and submit to registration at such time or times and place or places, and in such manner, as shall be determined by proclamation of the President and by rules and regulations prescribed hereunder."

Because the U.S. Constitution shows that the term natural born Citizen is different from Citizen of the United States, then this statute does not impose an artificial duty to register upon natural born Citizens, who naturally owe no artificial duties to Congress.

In particular, and under no circumstances, does the above statute apply to natural born Citizens residing outside of the United States. Admittedly, at most, this statute applies to natural born Citizens who reside within the United States.

However, 1) because the Equal Protection Clause of the 14th Amendment guarantees that natural born Citizens residing in the U.S. are to be treated the same as natural born Citizens residing outside the U..S. (because they are in the same class of persons), and 2) because natural born Citizens are not mentioned in the statute, then such natural law citizens residing in the United States are equally exempt from this statute. (We shall specifically discuss the Equal Protection Clause below.)

As natural law citizens, natural born Citizens are not naturally subject to positive law duty within a republic. They may not be lawfully required to register for anything, which is a duty imposed under equity upon artificial persons. Natural born Citizens have a natural political duty under law to defend their country in a war, but no artificial duty under equity to register with the positive law authority in advance of war. Otherwise they would be mentioned in the statute.

This discussion explains why these statutes are written as they are. Natural born Citizens are not mentioned because they are not inherently subject to artificial duties, such as the duty to register, which operate in equity.

Instead such citizens are subject only to natural political duties and the law jurisdiction 1) that secures natural born Citizens' natural political rights, such as liberty and the right to run for President, 2) that enforces natural political duties, such as the duty to defend the country, and 3) that adjudicates violations of natural rights in the form of torts and crimes.

We know that draft registration operates in equity, and is inapplicable to natural law citizens, for a couple of reasons. First, the statute refers solely to Citizens of the United States, which are positive law citizens, who are subject to positive political law. The statute excludes mention of natural born Citizens.

This is because positive law cannot legislate or create artificial duties that are applicable to natural law citizens. Republican legislatures can only write down or codify natural duties for natural citizens, but not create them.

Second, draft registration operates in equity because its punishment is equitable. 5 USC 3328 punishes male Citizens of the United States who fail to register for the draft by enjoining their future employment with the U.S. government.

Injunction is an equitable remedy, not a law remedy. Unless natural born Citizens have consented to equity, then they would not be subject to this equitable penalty in the statute.

This is to say that natural born Citizens are not enjoined from future government work for not registering for the draft because the statute does not apply to them. This is also to say that Congress may codify citizens' natural duties, such as the duty to defend one's country. However, it has no positive law authority to legislate legal duties upon natural born Citizens without them first giving their consent authority. 5 USC 3328 is an example of this.

If Congress required male natural born Citizens to register for the draft, then it could have 1) directly said so, or 2) called for the registration of all males with "the nationality of the United States...," as it refers to natural born Citizens, naturalized U.S. citizens, and nationals at 8 USC 1409(a) and (c). Given this, clearly Congress imposes no duty upon natural born Citizens to register for the draft.

Those male natural born Citizens who have registered for the draft have unnecessarily consented to the jurisdiction of Congress. Their registration is voluntary because the meaning of the above-cited statutes is unambiguous, i.e., they apply to Citizens of the United States, who are not natural born Citizens. Yet without being taught the meaning of their citizenship, or how to read statutes, then these false registrants thought they were subject to Congress, although they naturally were not.

This analysis is compatible with what has been established for a republic, i.e. that republican legislatures' positive law authority does not apply to natural persons, including natural law citizens, but only to artificial persons that the positive law created, including naturalized citizens and people residing in a country based on the national sovereign's permission.

This means that Congress and republican state legislatures may not legislate over (or may not legislate inconsistently with) natural born Citizens' natural inherited political rights. This includes the liberty to be free of a registration duty to an artificial political sovereign, without granting it one's consent. However, one has no natural liberty from the natural political duties 1) to not harm others, 2) to defend the political society from attack, 3) to report and witness torts and crimes, and 4) to serve as a juror in criminal judgment of one's peers.

A *Minor*, but curious citizenship glitch

Because there is no better place to briefly discuss the 15th and 19th Amendments to the U.S. Constitution, I have placed the discussion here. The 15th Amendment secured the right of non-whites and former slaves the right to vote in federal and state elections. The 19th Amendment did this for women.

In pertinent part, the 15th Amendment reads: "The right of Citizens of the United States to vote shall not be denied or abridged by the United States or any state on account of race, color or previous condition of servitude." The 19th Amendment did the same thing "on account of sex."

As previously mentioned, the 19th Amendment was precipitated by the case of *Minor v. Happersett* (1875) where the

Supreme Court held that Virginia Minor – a female natural born Citizen from Missouri – did not have a right to vote. [92] The Court negligently concluded this without discussing natural law, which is the source of natural born Citizens' right to vote in an American republic.

Given that Article II, Section 1, Clause 5 of the U.S. Constitution distinguishes natural born Citizens from Citizens of the United States, then the 15th and 19th Amendments do not apply to natural born Citizens. This is because such citizens are not mentioned in the amendments.

Instead, these amendments and the 14th Amendment apply to Citizens of the United States, who are not natural born Citizens. Thus the 14th, 15th and 19th Amendments did not change, increase or improve any rights of natural born Citizens.

These amendments granted no rights to natural born Citizens, and no additional rights particularly to non-white and female natural born Citizens. And thus, the 19th Amendment did not secure for natural born Citizen Virginia Minor – or any other female natural born Citizen – the right to vote. These amendments do not mention natural born Citizens, so do not affect the voting rights of any natural born Citizens.

So why are the 15th and 19th Amendments written as they are, i.e., to specifically apply to adopted Citizens of the United States? Were these drafting mistakes? Or were they strokes of clarity, only to be discerned by others like me years later?

My previous book on the false enforcement of drug laws in America [93] shows that the attorneys who write statutes and constitutional amendments tend to know law – which the U.S. Supreme Court calls the definition and limitation of power – better than most other attorneys.

In essence, they are superior attorneys because they understand the republican form of government (and all of its characteristics described herein), which others do not. My previous book shows how the Controlled Substances Acts were written by such attorneys so that few others would ever read and understand them, and so that most attorneys could be manipulated into falsely enforcing them, as they have for over fifty years.

This same superior type of attorneys wrote the 15th and 19th Amendments to exclude mention of non-white and female natural born Citizens. I presume that this was deliberate and that they did this:

1) because they knew that the Supreme Court's holding in *Minor v. Happersett* (1875) was wrong, i.e., incompatible with the republican form of government, in that the rights to vote and to run for President are not bestowed rights in an American republic, but instead are inherited natural rights which, based on natural political equality, belong to all natural born Citizens regardless of skin color or sex, and

2) because, given that the *Minor* Court had already shown itself to be unaware of the natural law jurisdiction in the U.S. Constitution, the amendments' authors figured that no one would likely ever notice that the constitution was never changed to grant Virginia Minor and all other non-white and female natural born Citizens the right to vote.

Readers who disagree with this analysis are equating the constitutional terms natural born Citizen with Citizen of the United States, which we have seen are opposite and opposed types of U.S. citizenship in the United States. This is to falsely equate bestowed political rights with natural inherited ones, and to fail to keep them separate, which is the essence of being nonrepublican.

Equating natural law- and positive law-citizenship is the only basis to claim that the 15th and 19th Amendments granted non-white and female natural born Citizens the right to vote. Because natural born and naturalized citizens are different classes of citizens, and because natural born Citizens are not mentioned in the 15th and 19th Amendments, then logically non-white and female natural born Citizens either 1) still do not have the rights to vote and to run for President, or 2) have the rights to vote and to politically participate as natural facts, just like their other natural rights under the U.S. Constitution.

Readers who still think that all rights come from government are required to confront, and cannot deny, the fact that the U.S. Constitution does not grant non-white and female natural born Citizens the right to vote. Thus voting and running for President by these people, for instance Hillary Clinton, 1) are either unlawful (unconstitutional) to attempt (because these activities exceed such persons' rights under the constitution), or instead 2) they have (and have always had) an unwritten natural political right to vote and to run for President, just like adult white male natural born Citizens.

The correct analysis compels recognition of the natural law jurisdiction and its political equality. The 15th and 19th Amendments are evidence – indeed admissions – that republics do not grant natural political rights to their natural law citizens, who are born with and inherit these natural rights equally.

(Reflective of the poor understanding of citizenship law – both then and now – Virginia Minor's attorney argued that her right to vote came from the 14th Amendment. Unaware of the natural law jurisdiction, neither he nor the Court realized that her right to vote was an unenumerated natural political right, secured by the 9th Amendment.)

If to vote and to run for President are natural political rights of natural born Citizens, then all such female citizens have had these rights since the nation was founded. As well, all such non-white citizens have had the right to vote and the right to create natural born Citizens at least since the 14th Amendment, which provided citizenship, due process and equal protection under the law to America's former slaves. Because some Americans resisted recognizing the right of non-white citizens to vote, then the 15th Amendment was also passed.

The points to remember from this section are 1) that the U.S. Supreme Court has long ignored or been unaware of the natural law jurisdiction in the U.S. Constitution, which is to be blind to how natural law defines such republican concepts as crime, marriage and natural born Citizens, and 2) that there are attorneys working for American governments – but not necessarily in the Supreme Court building – who understand the natural law basis of America's republican form of government, and who communicate their understanding via written positive law, which is often not understood by other American attorneys.

How do I know this? First-hand. The authors of the U.S. and Uniform Controlled Substances Acts, which I studied in order to write my previous book, [94] essentially both 1) taught me how to read cryptically-written statutes, and 2) taught or demonstrated to me all of the jurisdictional distinctions in republican law that I share in this book. Because law is to define and separate power, these authors literally taught me law, which I did not learn in law school.

I am also an eye-witness to the authors' fraudulent handiwork. Nearly fifty of my previous book's pages are used to decrypt the authors' intentionally misleading drug statutes, which could have instead been clearly written and organized so that republican justice would be fulfilled. [95] As we are learning, republican justice is achieved with regard to property 1) by recognizing individuals' right of property possession and 2) by regulating the commerce of property – even unwanted commerce – instead of treating it as criminally prohibited.

Nonetheless, unlike just about everyone else in the law business, the acts' authors demonstrate their knowledge of republican law by keeping separate all of the powers that are explained in this book. So do the authors of the 15th and 19th Amendments. One could not realize this without recognizing the role of natural law in the U.S. Constitution.

Because, as we have seen, these authors' properly-written statutes and constitutional amendments keep all republican powers separate, then this demonstrates their knowledge of republican law. Because practicing attorneys do not comprehend republican law and its separations of power as described

102

herein, then they have been unable to properly read these amendments and statutes.

Thus, just because these provisions were written to be republican by their authors who knew republican law, 1) does not mean that anyone understands them as such, or 2) does not mean that they are administered in republican fashion by officials and legal professionals who understand their roles – let alone their own citizenship – in America's republican form of government. This assessment goes for every attorney in America who does not understand the various separations of power that are described in this book.

The separation of science from opinion and belief

Another difference between law and equity relates to our prior discussion of what makes a republican government secular, and what makes all nonrepublican governments essentially religious. Governments are secular when their justice is based on objective natural science, and they are religious when their justice and "science" are based on subjective belief or opinion.

Monarchies are particularly religious because they are based on the unprovable belief or opinion that a supernatural god – by means of the backing of a major church – has chosen or ordained the national political sovereign.

But monarchies are not exceptional nonrepublics. All nonrepublics are based on one or more unprovable beliefs or opinions. Their primary unprovable proposition is that some people legitimately have superior moral authority to define other people's political rights, such as their rights to life, liberty, property, religion, and the pursuit of happiness.

As we have seen, this is both an unnatural and unprovable view, as well as a misrepresentation of republican law, which requires recognition of political equality under natural law. As torts and crimes in republics are defined by nature, then all people who unnaturally exert power over others, and violate their natural rights, are either tortfeasors or criminals.

This goes for government officials as for ordinary individuals. Torts and crimes are natural facts based on natural criteria, and are not subject to unprovable beliefs or opinions.

So when officials misrepresent this law, such as 1) by misrepresenting the power of legislatures to legislate (create) crime, or 2) by misrepresenting the exercise of certain rights as crimes, or 3) by denying the natural law basis of state and U.S. Constitutions, then naturally they are responsible for these misrepresentations, willful or not.

Officials cannot legitimately claim immunity to assert unequal, unnatural and undelegated power over other people, based on their beliefs and opinions. The Bill of Rights and the use of constitutional definitions of such terms as case, crime, natural born Citizen and property are meant to exclude all belief and opinion, including religious ones, from ruling individuals in their law jurisdiction.

Given this, because natural persons are not the subject matter of equity, then the Bill of Rights relates to securing natural persons' natural rights from the power of equity. That is, the Bill of Rights relates to securing natural persons from the jurisdiction of the legislative sovereign and from all of its beliefs and opinions. To avoid this subjectivity being applied to individuals is why the artificial political sovereign cannot legislate for or over the law jurisdiction, whose sovereign is nature and where the laws of nature define rights and wrongs.

Alas, the objectivity of nature's law jurisdiction protects individuals from the subjectivity of the sovereign in charge of equity. However, the Bill of Rights – which does not apply to artificial persons – is not intended to protect such artificial persons from being subject to such a subjective government.

The sovereign over artificial persons and the equity jurisdiction in a republic is the legislative sovereign, and such sovereign is characterized by belief and opinion. It is inherently subjective. So, the only way to protect individuals from a government based on belief and opinion – including religion – is to protect them from being subject to the legislative sovereign in the equity jurisdiction.

And that is what the separation of the judicial law jurisdiction from the equity jurisdiction of America's republics uniquely serves to do. However, it serves this purpose only for the benefit of natural persons – not artificial ones. There is no separation of power between legislatures and their creations.

The Bill of Rights which operates in the law jurisdiction helps maintain this separation by keeping the beliefs and opinions of the legislative sovereign from having any direct effect upon natural persons, who are subject instead to natural law, its morality, and its sciences. It does this by keeping the subject matter of the equity jurisdiction, i.e., artificial persons and their artificial rights, separate from the subject matter of the law jurisdiction, i.e., natural persons and their natural rights.

Because natural persons are not subject to equity, then they are not subject to any of the beliefs and opinions of republican legislatures, for example, that any kind of property possession is a crime. In the natural law jurisdiction, the opinions and beliefs of positive law authorities (legislatures, courts, administrators) have no direct effect because their positive law has no authority over what is natural, including over natural persons, over natural rights and wrongs, and over what is naturally true.

Truth and justice are secured in the law jurisdiction where right and wrong are adjudicated, where reality is defined naturally and scientifically, and where people's natural rights to form their own beliefs and opinions over their own lives and property are protected from the beliefs and opinions of others.

No legislative sovereign in the world has legitimate authority over natural persons that can be proven. Any power that legislatures assert over natural persons is strictly due to the sovereign's use of force or fraud, i.e., its forceful misrepresentations of legitimate power.

In the case of a nonrepublic, this fraud refers to the legislative sovereign's misrepresentation of superior natural power over less powerful people. In the case of a monarchy, it is the misrepresentation that God has ordained the monarch. In the case of a republic, any legislative claim over natural persons is strictly a misrepresentation of republican delegated power. To misrepresent willfully constitutes fraud.

In any case, the political sovereign's legitimate power over natural persons is unprovable. Other than with a strong fist or sleight of hand, nothing naturally proves that one person, or group of persons, is more equal than another.

For example, as we saw on pages 66 – 68, there is absolutely no proof that the Indiana legislature either can or has criminally prohibited any disfavored drug possession or commerce. Said differently, that drugs are criminally prohibited in the state of Indiana is not provable.

It is not provable by logic (natural law), constitutional law, statutory law or case law. As well, there are no regulations over drug possession because personal property possession is not subject to equity and its regulations within republics.

In fact, all of these types and layers of consistent law unanimously say that drug possession is lawful in Indiana and that drug dealing is regulated under equity. That drugs are criminally prohibited within Indiana, and that its legislature can define people's natural rights of liberty and property possession, are attorneys' subjective and unprovable opinions.

This in fact means that America's judicially-waged war on drugs is based solely on attorneys' mere opinions, and not on the existence or legitimacy of any natural, constitutional, statutory or case law. In America's republics, it is unconstitutional – by definition – for legislatures to determine the political rights of natural born Citizens in particular 1) because such rights are natural, granted by nature and defined by natural standards, and 2) because such power has not been delegated by the people to legislatures via the U.S. and state constitutions.

What makes a republican legislative sovereign less pow-

106

erful and less dangerous than a nonrepublican sovereign is that natural law and the natural rights of citizens are jurisdictional checks upon its positive-law authority in a republic. This check is maintained by keeping the natural subject matter of law (which answers to nature) separate from the artificial subject matter of equity (which answers to the political sovereign).

As we previously learned, the people's natural rights are reserved rights that they did not delegate to their republican governments. The Founding Fathers established the law jurisdiction to secure these rights from legislatures and to adjudicate violators of these natural rights using natural provable criteria. Likewise, they established the equity jurisdiction to administer positive law's artificial privileges and duties, albeit subjectively.

This is all to say that a subjective government of old, based on whimsical beliefs and opinions, is allowed to operate within the United States today. However, 1) it operates only in the equity jurisdiction of America's republics, 2) it is applicable only to artificial persons, who are creations of positive law, and 3) it is held in check from having any direct effect upon natural persons by the separation and operation of the law jurisdiction, to which they solely answer for their natural wrongs.

The law jurisdiction applies exclusively to natural persons and applies science instead of opinion. Tort and criminal liability are provable only by proving injury and its causation.

The legislative sovereign over equity may not define or redefine either elements of liability or natural truth in the law jurisdiction, which answers to natural law and its sciences. This arrangement defines the criteria upon which one may be compensated or incarcerated, i.e., injury, and scientifically secures natural persons' natural rights and duties.

Thus, science is enforced in the law jurisdiction and opinion and belief is enforced in equity. As we learned, the law jurisdiction enforces right and wrong using natural and objective criteria for justice, i.e., *malum in se*.

So *malum in se* is the basis of all legitimate tort and

criminal prosecutions in an American republic. Right and wrong under law are defined by the political laws of nature, based on injury, provable by science, and adjudicated in the law jurisdiction. This law jurisdiction is not subject to *malum prohibita*, 1) which operates solely under equity, 2) which is not about right and wrong, and 3) which is based on the beliefs and opinions of legislatures or their agents.

The religiosity of *malum prohibita* is held in check by individuals' natural right of conscience in the law jurisdiction, over which the legislature may not legislate. Under natural law, natural persons are not subject to legislative beliefs and opinions, have jurisdiction over their own consciences, and are lawfully responsible only for violating their natural duties to others.

Thus, the law jurisdiction is the secular force and face of American republican government, which is based upon natural, objective and verifiable science. On the other hand, the equity jurisdiction is not the jurisdiction of objective right and wrong, but is that characterized by the beliefs and opinions of the political sovereign.

Equity is the opinionated face of American government, 1) whose natural authority to legislate over individuals' political rights is unprovable and 2) whose real authority is based solely a) upon the delegation of the people's power. and b) upon the consent of otherwise free people.

Thus in America's republics, the authority to enforce opinion and belief is strictly confined to the equity jurisdiction. Subjective, artificial definitions such as *malum prohibita* apply only to artificial persons, who are subject to non-criminal sanctions under equity.

This makes *malum prohibita* essentially legislative and regulatory opinion. It has nothing to do with right and wrong, which is defined by nature and enforced in the law jurisdiction.

This positive law opinion need not be proven by facts or logic. It answers only to a subjective sovereign. Fortunately in a republic, such opinion does not apply to individuals, whose justice system operates in a separate jurisdiction from equity.

This is all to show that opinion and belief, such as religion, is prohibited in the law jurisdiction where individuals' natural rights are secured by the Bill of Rights. However, it is not prohibited in the legislative world of equity. The American People granted power to legislatures only over commerce, immigration and governmental affairs, but not over the natural law jurisdiction of individuals, which defines their rights to life, liberty and personal property.

The nation's Founding Fathers realized that legislatures acting subjectively and by opinion can be downright dangerous. This is why they granted legislative power only over artificial persons who consent to be governed in equity.

To know what is opinion and what is science is essential knowledge for all legal practitioners, students of political science, and conscientious citizens. Only with this knowledge can one know the distinctions between law and equity, between prohibition and regulation, and between criminal and administrative law within America's republican form of government.

In contrast, nonrepublics enforce only opinion. Nature and its objective sciences are nonrepublics' natural political enemies. By definition, nonrepublican justice is based upon supernatural claims of power and upon Man's subjectivity.

In nonrepublics, there are no immutable standards for justice because such governments deny nature's role in governing. And as we shall see, there is no separation of powers in nonrepublics because all governmental authority serves the sole political sovereign – and not necessarily its subjects.

In contrast, in republics – where natural law defines political rights – then it is self-evident that all citizens have equal political rights in the law jurisdiction. Criminal and citizenship standards are based upon natural and objective criteria instead of upon the subjectivity of Man.

To adopt the nonrepublican form of government is to deny natural reality that all people are created equal. It is instead to claim that a monarch or legislature can define natural reality, including the scope of other people's rights, which in republics are natural facts.

Because the nonrepublican form of government denies natural reality, for example that all people are created equal, then it is a form of insanity. In contrast, because the republican form of government recognizes natural reality, such as natural political equality, then it is the only form of government that is sane. Because republican governments are exclusively sane, then sane people should exclusively embrace this form.

In conclusion, the law jurisdiction is secular and based on science. It defines crime, citizenship, marriage and property, for example, naturally and objectively. It is the science of law in the law jurisdiction that makes republican governments secular.

In contrast, the equity jurisdiction is based on opinion and belief. It operates by the laws of Man – and not by the laws of nature – just like all parts of nonrepublics.

Without the natural law jurisdiction, all elements of government would be based upon belief and opinion embodied in positive law, operating in equity, whose sovereign is political. Without the natural law jurisdiction, then there would be no check upon the authority of positive law. Without natural law as the basis of criminal law and citizenship, then America's legislatures would subjectively define citizens' political rights.

Thus, the republican form of government is one whose judicial law jurisdiction is based on science and whose equity jurisdiction allows for legislative and judicial beliefs and opinions (although we might wish that it would not).

The law and equity sides of equal protection

Above, we defined the differences between judicial due process of law and administrative due process. The former is a substantive right of a natural person, defined by republican constitutions and enforceable in the law jurisdiction. The latter applies to artificial persons under equity, as defined by statute.

As we have seen, the 14th Amendment says that all persons – both natural and artificial persons – are owed due process. Due process of law for natural persons is defined in the law jurisdiction by the Bill of Rights, which secures their natural constitutional rights. Administrative due process is owed to artificial persons in the adjudication of their legal rights.

In addition to due process, the 14th amendment says that both natural and artificial persons are also owed equal protection. Equal protection means that republics must treat persons who are in the same class with the same due process.

The U.S. Supreme Court in *Truax v. Corrigan* (1921) [96] wrote that equal protection "means that no person or class of persons shall be denied the same protection of the laws which is enjoyed by other persons or other classes in the same place and under like circumstances."

This statement of law obviously assumes that there are different classes of persons in the United States. There are three class distinctions cited below. This would necessarily mean that the U.S. is not a classless society.

As we have seen, the first class distinction is whether a person is natural or artificial. Republics are to treat all natural persons with due process of law, and are to treat all artificial persons within administrative due process.

The former process is judicial, operating in the law jurisdiction and defined by constitutions. The latter process is administrative, primarily operating in the executive branch, and defined by the legislative sovereign. Natural and artificial persons are not the same and are not equal.

With regard to all artificial commercial persons, equal protection is to treat persons in the same class equally. Thus all gun sellers, all drug manufacturers, all pig farmers, all gas refineries, and all supermarkets, for example, are to be given the same respective treatment from government as other enterprises in their category.

111

Thus, for example, disfavored drug dealers are to be afforded the same administrative due process as favored ones who operate in the pharmaceutical industry. All enterprises that manufacture, distribute or dispense drugs are to register with state drug regulators and with the D.E.A. Some of these drug dealers will meet the standards of these regulators. Others will not.

But nonetheless, America's republics are required to provide all drug dealers – both the good kind and the bad kind – with equal administrative due process. Those who do not meet regulators' standards, or who have not attempted to register, are subject to commercial property confiscation and can be administratively enjoined from dealing drugs. To enjoin means to order someone to stop doing something.

In America's republics, such injunction is first ordered by a regulatory agency under its equitable powers. [97] If compliance is not achieved administratively, then such order can be made by a judicial court, with the power to incarcerate a party for judicial contempt. [98] Thus, that *malum prohibita* which cannot be enforced at the administrative level, for example by means of an administrative injunction, can ultimately be addressed by judicial forfeiture and injunction proceedings.

A second class distinction is that between U.S. citizens and foreigners. All U.S. citizens have a right under the U.S. Constitution to be within the United States, but foreigners do not. Instead, their political right to be in the country is subject to Congress, who today treats unregistered foreigners as *malum prohibita*. More on this in the next section.

A third class distinction is that all U.S. citizens are not equal. Naturalized Citizens of the United States, who are characterized by having alien fathers, are in a different class of citizens than natural born Citizens, who have citizen fathers.

Naturalized citizens 1) owe political duties to Congress which natural born Citizens do not, and 2) may not run or serve as President or Vice President, which offices are reserved for natural born Citizens.

These are two of the differences between natural and positive law U.S. citizens. Equal protection means to treat all natural born Citizens the same and to treat all Citizens of the United States the same, as they each are in separate classes.

Because all adopted citizens are natural law aliens, then they have no natural right to be U.S. President. Because torts and crimes are violations of natural rights, thus it is not a tort or a crime to deny Citizens of the United States such a right.

To sum things up, both due process and equal protection are owed to both natural and artificial persons. And thus, due process and equal protection operate under both law and equity. Both natural and artificial persons are to receive their own form of due process, which is equal among their class or category.

That equal protection was not mentioned in the U.S. Constitution until the 14th Amendment was ratified is for good reason. Natural persons already had natural political equality under natural political law as a substantive right in the (natural) law jurisdiction of judicial courts. The amendment reminds us that while foreigners are artificial persons under equity, they are also natural persons under law.

This equality under law is achieved by guaranteeing due process of law, which is predominantly defined by the Bill of Rights. It also includes the substantive right to rely on the natural and constitutional meaning of such words as crime, offense, felony, misdemeanor, and natural born Citizen.

The 14th Amendment was intended to shore up equality for adopted citizens and other artificial persons, which right cannot be alienated from any natural law citizen or person. The "best principles [of our republic] secure to all its citizens a perfect equality of rights," wrote Thomas Jefferson. [99]

For natural persons, equality before the law is a substantive right. For artificial persons, equal protection is achieved by regulating members of the same artificial class with the same administrative due process. This administrative process operates under equity, primarily in the executive branch.

Regulators' equitable powers include the power to investigate, confiscate from and enjoin unwanted commercial activity, i.e., *malum prohibita*. This executive branch authority precludes the judicial branch of government from having subject matter jurisdiction over the same activity. A judicial system remains republican so long as it separates power between the law and equity jurisdictions based on subject matter.

The separation of regulation from prohibition

The separation of law from equity as we discussed in the five prior sections is carried out by separating the roles of the two police powers in a republic: regulation and criminal prohibition. So far we have learned 1) that regulation operates in equity over artificial persons, and 2) that crimes are what is naturally prohibited by natural persons, i.e., *malum in se.*

Our analysis has revealed that these two separate republican police powers operate in separate branches of government (judicial and executive), in separate judicial jurisdictions (law and equity), and over different kinds of persons, subject matter and rights (natural and artificial). Given this background, below we will better note the distinctions between criminal prohibition and regulation.

Criminal prohibition operates in the law jurisdiction of the judicial branch, assisted by law enforcers (police officers and prosecutors) in the executive branch. Regulation operates administratively, or non-judicially, primarily in administrative law courts in the executive branch, with ultimate enforcement authority in the judicial branch.

Criminal prohibition enforces the law of the natural sovereign and operates upon natural persons. Regulation enforces the positive law of a legislative sovereign and operates upon artificial persons.

Thus, prohibition operates at law, in the law jurisdiction

114

of the judicial branch. Regulation operates under equity in the executive branch.

Prohibition adjudicates violations of one's natural duties to others, which are violations to others' natural rights. Regulation adjudicates legal rights and duties of artificial persons.

Prohibition has subject matter jurisdiction over injury to others, which are *malum in se*. Regulation has jurisdiction over commerce, foreigners and government administration.

Legislatures have authority to proscribe (or prohibit) disfavored commercial behavior, such as drug dealing, and classes of artificial persons, such as aliens. These legislative prohibitions are *malum prohibita*. However, legislatures have no authority to define or legislate what is good and what is *malum in se* for individuals, which are naturally defined.

Thus, *malum in se* is injurious individual behavior that violates other people's rights, while *malum prohibita* is commercial behavior or foreign people that are disfavored by a legislative sovereign. The former is subject to civil or criminal prohibition under law, while the latter is subject to regulation under equity.

Said differently, *malum in se* is that which is naturally prohibited by the political laws of nature and adjudicated in the law jurisdiction of judicial courts. On the other hand, *malum prohibita* is that which is artificially prohibited by the legislature, as enforced by regulators.

Injured parties and prosecutors (on their behalf) prosecute *malum in se* in the judicial branch. The remedies available in the law jurisdiction include civil damages and incarceration. In contrast, as we have seen, regulators use the equitable powers of forfeiture and injunction to fight *malum prohibita*.

The U.S. Supreme Court in *Ohio v. Helvering* (1934) told us that the police power with regard to commerce is regulatory. It wrote: "Nevertheless, the police power is and remains a governmental power, and, applied to business activities, is the power to regulate those activities..." [100]

This means that all commerce within a republic (except for the trafficking of people) is subject to regulation under equity – and that it is not subject to criminal prohibition under law.

As we have seen, in an American republic, that which is inherently wrong or *malum in se* is naturally prohibited in the law jurisdiction of the judicial branch. Thus, the police power of criminal prohibition applies to that which is naturally bad, which is behavior that harms other people.

As we have also seen, that behavior which is merely proscribed by a legislature, i.e., its *malum prohibita*, does not apply to natural persons, does not create natural duties in them, and is not enforced in the law jurisdiction, which is a republic's only criminal authority. *Malum prohibita* is enforced under equity, primarily using administrative law courts in the executive branch, applicable only to artificial persons.

So, *malum in se* is naturally prohibited behavior, which is enforced as civil or criminal actions in the judicial branch. In contrast, *malum prohibita* is legislatively disfavored behavior by artificial persons, such as business people and foreigners, who are regulated in the executive branch under non-criminal equity.

Thus, that behavior which is bad by its nature is naturally prohibited by civil or criminal law, and is the subject matter of the law jurisdictions. In all cases the jurisdiction of law courts requires the averment of an injury-in-fact. Criminally, an exception to this constitutional requirement can be achieved only by amending America's constitutions.

In contrast, that behavior which is artificial in nature is subject to the will of positive law, as enforced by regulatory agencies. This means that such behavior is not subject to criminal law, which is outside of the legislature's sovereign authority.

Consequently, that behavior which is neither injurious to others nor legislatively regulated is subject neither to prohibition nor regulation. It is behavior that is therefore ungoverned and not subject to positive law.

Because only that which is naturally bad is subject to the law jurisdiction, then a constitutional amendment is needed to change the subject matter jurisdiction of judicial courts. For example, the 18th Amendment to the U.S. Constitution took the commerce of alcohol – its manufacture, transportation and dispensing – out of the equity jurisdiction where it had been subject to non-criminal regulation, and placed it into the law jurisdiction where it could be treated as a crime.

For Alcohol Prohibition to end, the 21st Amendment took alcohol commerce out of the law jurisdiction where it was subject to criminal prosecution, and placed the commercial activity back into equity, where it is regulated.

A constitutional amendment was needed to prohibit alcohol commerce 1) because natural persons could only be put in jail in the law jurisdiction, 2) because natural criminal law does not naturally proscribe any consensual commercial behavior, such as buying or selling alcohol, and 3) because all commerce in a republic (except that in slaves, which is *malum in se*) is subject to the non-criminal equity jurisdiction, and not to the criminal law jurisdiction.

(Parenthetically, the 18th amendment did not change or diminish anyone's natural, unalienable right to possess or drink alcohol during Prohibition. According to U.S. law, alcohol possession was lawful during Alcohol Prohibition, just as was drug possession then (and now)).

So, it took a constitutional amendment to remove alcohol commerce from regulation under equity and to place it into the criminal law jurisdiction, where nature normally defines crime. Said differently, it took a constitutional amendment to treat legislatures' *malum prohibita* against alcohol commerce as *malum in se*, the latter which is the natural subject matter of republican criminal courts.

Due to its voluntary nature, the making and dispensing of alcohol to consenting adults is not a crime under the natural law jurisdiction of the U.S. Constitution. Because of this, America's republican constitutions require amendments to treat artificial prohibitions (*malum prohibita*) as natural ones (*malum in se*).

Cconstitutional amendments are required in order to move any kind of subject matter from one jurisdiction to another. This applies to all the various separations of powers that are discussed in this book.

The difference between regulation and criminal prohibition is also illustrated by the institution of slavery and the 13th Amendment, which criminally proscribed it. Prior to the Civil War, slavery was criminally prohibited in the northern states and regulated in equity in the south. In the south, there was a constitutionally-imposed excise tax on slaves, and their importation and exportation became *malum prohibita* after 1811.

In contrast, in the north, it was considered *malum in se* – or a violation of natural law – for one natural person to own another. Indiana's 1816 constitution condemned slavery as "usurpation and tyranny." [101] In the northern states, slavery was criminally prohibited except as punishment for crime. [102]

After the Civil War, the 13th Amendment took former slaves, who were considered property (or chattel) in the southern states and in the federal areas, out of being the subjects of regulation, and elevated them to natural persons under law.

The use and trade in slaves were no longer regulated, but became universally prohibited – as *malum in se* – within all the states of the union. The 13th Amendment prohibited slavery and indentured servitude except as punishment for the commission of crime, naturally defined.

The 13th Amendment took former slaves out of regulation and placed them under law, or natural law. There they could still be enslaved, but only for the same reason as other natural persons, i.e., for committing crimes.

As we shall see, because crime is defined as *malum in se* by natural law, it ensures natural freedom as an equal natural right to all who do not violate the rights of others. The 13th Amendment guaranteed everyone's liberty unless they committed a *malum in se* crime.

These examples of the 13th, 18th and 21st Amendments illustrate the roles of republics' two police powers: criminal prohibition and regulation. Criminal prohibition applies only to that which is *malum in se* (inherently wrong) or to that which is placed into the criminal law jurisdiction of judicial courts by constitutional amendments. Otherwise, regulation applies to all commerce.

Ultimately, when a person is not regulated and when that person carries on his affairs without harming other people, then that person is free both from equity and the law jurisdictions of government. In such capacity within a republic, one is essentially free in the state of nature.

Federalism, part 1: The separation of U.S. from state powers

As law is the definition and limitation of power, the term federalism is the proper definition or separation of power between the states and Congress. As we introduced above, Congress legislates in two capacities.

First, it legislates as a republic over particular subject matter that occurs within the state republics. Second, it legislates in a local or municipal capacity over its own land, water and air realm, called the federal areas. So, federalism defines the power of Congress in these two capacities as these two powers relate to the states.

As a republic, Congress 1) regulates interstate commerce within the states under authority of the Commerce Clause at Article I, Section 8, Clause 3 of the U.S. Constitution, 2) regulates foreigners within the states under authority of Article I, Section 8, Clause 4, and 3) has a handful of federal criminal powers there as well. As republics, Congress and the states share the same republican meaning of case and crime, defined by injury.

On the other hand, Congress legislates as a nonrepublic with regard to its own federal areas. This is under authority of Article I, Section 8, Clause 17 of the U.S. Constitution. Suffice here to say that as a nonrepublic, it does not treat people in the federal areas as natural persons to which the Bill of Rights and due process of law fully apply (if at all).

Because the states and Congress treat commercial persons and foreign persons within the states as artificial persons, both which exist in the United States by privilege of positive law, then both classes of artificial persons are owed administrative due process in these regulatory matters.

As natural persons, aliens are owed due process of law in the law jurisdiction of judicial courts with regard to tort and criminal cases. State and U.S. criminal law enforcers must provide foreigners, who are natural persons, with due process of law when charging them with crimes.

This means that in the United States, foreign persons are subject to nature and to its criminal prohibitions just as are Americans. This also means that under the (natural) law jurisdiction, their rights are equal to Americans. Within the states they can be imprisoned only for crimes, naturally defined.

However, not only are foreigners in the U.S. subject to the criminal law jurisdiction, which upholds their natural duties to others, they are also subject to Congress, which U.S. citizens are normally not. The powers of Congress over foreigners and over immigration and naturalization do not apply in particular to natural born Citizens. However, Congress' power can be enforced amongst such citizens – that is, within their states – against the artificial persons to which Congress' powers apply.

As artificial persons within the states, foreigners are subject to Congress' artificial regulatory jurisdiction under equity, just like commercial persons are. In this capacity, Congress and the states owe them administrative due process

As we have seen, administrative due process is legislatively defined and owed to artificial persons in administrative courts. This is in contrast to due process of law which is defined by the Bill of Rights and is owed in the law jurisdiction to all natural persons, including foreigners.

As we have discussed throughout this book, there are two forms of government in this world, i.e., republican and non-republican. The above paragraphs exist to show that both forms of government operate within the United States, over separate areas and over separate subject matter.

That is, Congress legislates in two capacities. It legislates both as a republic with regard to the states and as an dictatorial nonrepublic with regard to the federal areas, including all U.S. navigable waterways, ships and airplanes.

This means that, depending upon where within the United States one is (for example, standing in Maryland or flying in a commercial airliner), then either a) one is entitled to a republican form of government, or b) one is a subject of the sole American nonrepublic.

That is, wherever one is within the United States, either the republican or nonrepublican form of government applies to that person – but not both forms at the same time, over the same subject matter. This is because of the first rule of law that we learned at the beginning of this book, i.e., that there is only one sovereign over any particular property, territory or activity.

Thus, wherever one is within the United States, one is under either a republican or a nonrepublican government. One must know this to navigate one's rights, to properly read U.S. statutes, or to properly represent law and legal clients.

The separation of U.S. and state regulatory powers

Given this background, we will devote our attention in the next two sections to pillar No. 1 of federalism, i.e., how Congress and the states – each as republics – separate their republican police powers of criminal prohibition and regulation, as well as their republican judicial powers of law and equity. Hereunder we will essentially define – briefly but with exactness – the subject matter over which states and Congress are respectively sovereign.

As noted in the previous sections, there are two police powers in a republic: criminal prohibition and regulation. Let us begin with a discussion of the latter, i.e., of the separation of power between the states' regulatory authority and that of Congress within the states. Each government's regulatory power operates in equity and is primarily exercised in its executive branch.

There are two objects of regulation that we will discuss below: i.e., the regulation of commercial activity and the regulation of foreigners (aliens) within the state republics. Likely the form and extent of both of these types of regulation are different than that envisioned by the Founding Fathers.

For example, I doubt that most founders could have dreamed 1) that commercial regulation would include wholesale property confiscation, under governments' powers of forfeiture, or 2) that Congress' power to regulate interstate commerce would be judged to include exclusively intrastate commerce. [103]

Nor perhaps could they have imagined all of the federal agencies created on behalf or because of foreigners, such as the Department of Homeland Security (D.H.S.), the U.S. Immigration and Customs Enforcement (I.C.E.), the U.S. Citizenship and Immigration Services (U.S.C.I.S.), the U.S. Customs and Border Protection (C.B.P.), along with U.S. immigration courts.

With regard to regulation of commere and foreigners, the states and Congress have always shared this authority in some manner. Congress' power to regulate interstate commerce is expressed in the aforementioned Interstate Commerce clause. [104] Its regulatory power over foreigners stems from the Naturaliztion clause.[105]

These concurrent state and U.S. regulatory powers

operate upon people only in their artificial commercial or foreign capacities. For example, republics regulate manufacturers, distributors and dispensers of goods and services, but they do not regulate personal production, purchases and consumption, which operate in the natural law jurisdiction. Likewise, they regulate foreigners but not natural born Citizens.

So, both state legislatures and Congress are constitutionally empowered to regulate commerce and foreigners on behalf of the public. Their power to regulate is concurrent. When conflicts occur, the U.S. Supremacy Clause [106] deems U.S. regulatory authority to be superior to that of the states. [107]

For example, many states currently allow the sale of cannabis through regulated dispensers. However, Congress and its regulators in the D.E.A. treat such interstate cannabis commerce as *malum prohibita*.

Under federal regulatory law, the D.E.A. – as the supreme drug regulator – has authority to confiscate the growing-equipment, cannabis produce and proceeds from the sale of cannabis of state licensees. Its interstate regulatory power over *malum prohibita* is superior to a state's power to protect the commerce of its cannabis licensees.

That the D.E.A. does not assert its superior power is not an issue in federalism, which is jurisdictional. It is not an issue over the separation of power between the states and Congress.

Further, it is not an issue over whether a state or the federal government has superior authority over cannabis commerce. *Gonzales v. Raich* (2005) upheld federal regulatory supremacy even in the most private, most intrastate of commercial transactions. [108]

The D.E.A.'s inaction is instead an issue of conflicting regulatory policies over cannabis, not disagreements over power. Disagreements over power are constitutional issues, with the Supreme Court as chief arbitrator. Disputes over policy are political.

Both Congress and the states agree that Congress' power

123

over cannabis commerce is superior. However they do not share the same opinion, belief or policy that cannabis should be distributed. In such a conflict, and when federal regulators seek to assert their power over those of the states, then Congress' regulatory police power displaces that of the states.

That the D.E.A. has not shut down and confiscated the commercial property of state cannabis licensees is strictly an exercise of discretion, and not because Congress is limited in its power to shut down interstate *malum prohibita*, regardless what the states permit.

As we learned earlier, these regulatory powers are non-criminal powers. On behalf of republics, the regulators of both the states and Congress have equitable powers to confiscate, get forfeited and enjoin unwanted commercial *malum prohibita*.

However, these equitable regulatory powers do not include the power to incarcerate natural persons, which latter power operates in the law jurisdiction of the judicial branch.

The regulation of immigration works in much the same manner as the regulation of commerce, in that Congress has supreme regulatory authority. Its powers over immigration and naturalization are defined at Article I, Section 8, Clause 4 of the U.S. Constitution.

However, compared with the regulation of commerce, 1) states play a much smaller role in regulating immigrants than the federal government does, and 2) both state judicial and Article III courts are required to treat all immigrants, both documented and undocumented, as natural persons, subject to the Bill of Rights, including due process of law.

This means that immigrants are to be treated by the law jurisdiction of the judicial system as natural persons who cannot be arrested – just like other natural persons – except for the commission of *malum in se* crime. Nonetheless they are subject to non-criminal regulation under equity for being foreigners, just as business people are subject to regulation for being in commerce.

Thus, foreigners are accorded the Bill of Rights to secure their natural rights as natural persons in judicial courts, just like Americans, but are nonetheless subject to regulation for having consented to the jurisdiction of Congress as aliens. This is analogous to a natural born Citizen being owed due process under the Bill of Rights, yet being owed only administrative due process when acting as a licensed driver or businessperson.

In *Wong Wing v. United States* (1896) the Supreme Court ruled that: "The Fourteenth Amendment to the constitution is not confined to the protection of citizens." [109] As we have seen, the 14th Amendment applies to states' treatment of both natural persons and artificial persons, such as foreign persons.

For foreigners as natural persons, the 14th Amendment secures due process of law in state republican courts, where the natural rights of foreigners can be secured. Similarly, Congress also recognizes foreigners' standing as natural persons in federal tort claims which are based on injury. [110]

However, unlike natural born Citizens, foreigners do not have a natural right to be within the United States. Instead they exercise a privilege that is grantable by Congress. As such, they exist within the United States as both natural and artificial persons, who are subject not only to the law jurisdiction as natural persons, but subject also to the U.S. equity jurisdiction as foreign, artificial persons.

Thus, foreigners within the United States have natural rights that are secured in the law jurisdiction of the judicial branch, all the while having artificial duties (and rights to administrative due process) under equity – just as if they were regulated as business people. And if foreigners earn income and become subject to the U.S. income tax system, then they are regulated under both the Taxing and Naturalization clauses of the U.S. Constitution. [111]

Congress regulates all foreigners as it may all interstate commercial persons. For example, as all commercial persons who manufacture, distribute and dispense controlled substances are required to register with the D.E.A. as the federal drug regulator, all foreigners over fourteen years of age are required to register with the Department of Homeland Security. These requirements to register are, again, because all foreigners and people engaged in interstate commerce are regulated.

Drug dealers and foreigners over fourteen years old who do not respectively register with the D.E.A. or the D.H.S. are *malum prohibita*. They are outlawed in equity, but not at law.

This is because they are not *malum in se* – evil by their nature, which is to be *unlawful* and subject to the law jurisdiction of state or U.S. courts. Instead they are *illegal* solely according to the legislative sovereign, which determines what is legal under equity, but not what is lawful under law. Recall that what is legal and what is lawful have separate sovereigns, i.e. Man and nature.

Whether for documented or undocumented foreigners, removal proceedings are conducted in U.S. immigration courts, which are administrative law courts. Their adjudications may be appealed to the Board of Immigration Appeal in the Executive Office for Immigration Review (EOIR). [112]

Deportation orders by these U.S. immigration courts are in the nature of equitable orders of specific performance. They are based on foreigners' explicit or implied agreement to obtain Congress' permission to be within the United States.

Many current deportation orders grant deportees time before being deported. Those aliens who fail to comply with such orders, by not showing up for their transportation home, are deemed to be fugitives, in contempt of court, and are subject to being physically detained and deported.

Thus, these non-criminal orders against foreigners are enforced by the exercise of contempt authority by U.S. courts, just like injunctions are against unwanted drug dealers. Neither drug dealers nor immigrants are criminals under the law jurisdiction which adjudicates *malum in se*. Instead both are subject to regulatory agencies that ultimately and respectively

126

can throw them in jail or out of the country for being in contempt of court orders.

The law jurisdiction has no authority over foreigners unless they commit torts or crimes. Thus, foreigners by their honest and nonviolent nature may be lawful, which term refers to behavior in the natural law jurisdiction that is not *malum in se*. However, these same foreigners may be illegal (which correct term refers to their lack of artificial rights to be within the United States), which privileges operate under equity.

So, undocumented immigrants may be both lawful and yet illegal. They may be peaceful and honest, and thus compliant with natural law. Yet they may be unregistered and in violation of positive law, i.e., *malum prohibita*.

This works the same way for business people in publicly disfavored commerce, for instance prostitution. Prostitution is lawful in that it is voluntary and consensual, but it may be considered illegal, i.e., *malum prohibita*, by a health department. Thus, it is behavior that can be enjoined, but not criminalized by a republican legislature.

Again, this is because the words *law* and *legal* operate in separate judicial jurisdictions. People's lawfulness is defined by natural law in the law jurisdiction. Their legality is defined by their compliance with positive law duties imposed by an artificial sovereign, which do not apply to natural persons.

Foreigners have the same rights under nature and its law jurisdiction as citizens do. However they are duty bound under equity because their status in the United States is privileged and not a natural right.

Relevant to this discussion is the scope of state regulatory authority over immigrants. As with states' regulation of commerce, states' regulation of foreigners is subject to congressional pre-emption based on the Supremacy Clause.

A case in point is Arizona's immigration law, the so-called Arizona Senate Bill 1070. Among other things, this act 1) required all foreigners over fourteen years old in Arizona to register with the state, just as they are to register under federal law, 2) instituted immigration status checks during law enforcement stops, and 3) criminalized foreigners for not carrying proof of registration.

In the case of *Arizona v. United States* (2012) the U.S. Supreme Court upheld the state provision that required status checks during law enforcement stops, but struck down the other provisions as violations of the Supremacy Clause. One of these provisions was the state's criminalization of foreigners who failed to carry registration papers.

This particular provision is relevant to our discussion because readers now know 1) that nature defines crimes within state republics, not legislatures, 2) that because foreigners are subject to registration, this means that they are subject to the equity jurisdiction, which is non-criminal, and 3) that within a republic, no individual may be arrested for a regulatory violation (because regulation and prohibition operate in separate judicial jurisdictions).

Thus, this state criminal provision constitutionally failed not merely because the Supremacy Clause preempted it (which raises another issue, to be discussed below), but because the provision violates the republican form of government. Republics can only arrest criminals, not regulation violators – not even if they are foreign.

In the republican form of government, all crimes are defined by nature, and such definition is applied to all natural persons equally. All foreigners and citizens – as natural persons – are owed due process of law and the other Bill of Rights in the law jurisdiction. Redundantly, these rights are secured for foreigners and positive law citizens by the 14th Amendment.

Because of the Separation of Powers Doctrine, republics are not allowed to criminalize violations of regulatory duties, such as the duty of a foreigner to register or to carry papers. Foreigners, like citizens, can be arrested for their actions only when they harm other people.

In any event, both commerce and foreigners are regulated in the United States. Congress has supreme regulatory power over both. Unlike natural born Citizens, both commercial activity and foreigners exist in the United States by permission of the legislative sovereign, and are subject to it.

This is all to say that Congress may declare unwanted commerce and unwanted foreigners as *malum prohibita*, and subject them to equitable remedies such as injunction and specific performance. However, neither Congress nor a state legislature may declare them to be criminal. This is because nature – and not legislatures – determines what is unlawful in a republic.

Foreigners are not *malum in se* – bad by their nature. However, unwanted foreigners may be made *malum prohibita*, and subject to government's equitable powers of deportation.

The separation of U.S. and state criminal powers

In contrast to Congress' interstate power to regulate commerce and foreigners, which is the supreme regulatory authority over this subject matter within the states, Congress' police power of criminal prohibition is much more limited within the territory of the fifty United States.

First, the general rule is that criminal jurisdiction is territorial. "Criminal law is usually territorial," reads a report from the Congressional Research Service. Usually crime "is a matter of the law of the place where it occurs." [113] With only the four exceptions noted below, criminal authority over acts committed within the states lies almost exclusively under the states' authority.

That is, almost all crimes that are committed within the borders of each state are state crimes, where the laws of Congress and the apparatus of the federal government are not primarily applicable. The four main exceptions to this rule or phenomenon are granted to Congress via the U.S. Constitution.

The first exception to otherwise-exclusive state criminal

jurisdiction within the states is Congress' criminal authority over a handful of federal crimes listed at Article I, Section 8 of the U.S. Constitution. These enumerated federal crimes are those crimes that occur anywhere within the United States over which federal law enforcers and U.S. Article III courts have primary criminal jurisdiction.

These federal enumerated crimes, which are each listed in Article I, Section 8 of the U.S. Constitution include 1) the counterfeiting of securities and currency of the United States, [114] 2) piracy, [115] 3) felonies on the high seas, [116] 4) "Offenses against the Laws of Nations," [117] and perhaps insurrections. [118]

So, for example, if pirates navigate a river to pillage a state, or if criminals defraud others with counterfeit currency within a state, or if people reveal government secrets to the nation's enemies from within a state, then the U.S. government has exclusive jurisdiction over these enumerated crimes within the states. Federal criminal power displaces state criminal power over these particular crimes. [119]

The second exception of state authority over crimes is a category of crimes called "offenses against the United States." It is possible that this category of crime belongs in the above-mentioned category of "Offenses against the Laws of Nations."

In any event, offenses against the United States include, but are not limited to: 1) giving away state secrets, 2) violating the Postal Privilege [120], which is the privilege to use U.S. mail, and 3) damaging U.S. property.

An example of the latter is the case of Timothy McVeigh and Terry Nichols for their participation in the Oklahoma City bombing in 1995. Although McVeigh and Nichols could have been charged with 168 state counts of murder, they were instead charged with offending the United States. [121] This gave the U.S. government criminal jurisdiction over their mass murder.

However, had McVeigh or Nichols instead gone inside the Murrah Federal Building and murdered some people, these acts would have solely been Oklahoma crimes, and could not have been charged as offenses against the U.S. This is because states retain criminal jurisdiction over federal buildings unless the criminal offends the United States, or unless the state has ceded criminal jurisdiction over that property to Congress, as discussed directly below.

The third exception to state criminal authority over crimes occurring within their borders is one previously mentioned (and noted directly above). The U.S. government has criminal jurisdiction within the borders of the states in those particular areas, called the federal areas or enclaves, 1) which Congress has acquired through purchase and 2) over which the states have ceded criminal jurisdiction.

This territorial variety of federal jurisdiction within the states is explained in a two-volume U.S. government publication entitled *Report on Jurisdiction Over Federal Areas Within The States.* [122] This report applies to all land, buildings and other property owned by Congress within the states, and explains the power that Congress exercises in them.

Essentially the report says that – with the exception of several federal crimes related to Congress' enumerated powers and to offenses against the United States, both which we discussed above – then Congress has legislative (and thus, criminal) jurisdiction within states only 1) over land that it owns and 2) over land to which a state has ceded either partial or exclusive legislative jurisdiction.

The report shows that legislative jurisdiction within state republics is acquired by Congress through state consent statutes and cession laws. As Article I, Section 8, Clause 17 of the U.S. Constitution explains, U.S. legislative jurisdiction – and thus, U.S. criminal jurisdiction – extends to "all Places purchased by the Consent of the Legislature of the State in which the Same shall be..."

The degree of U.S. legislative jurisdiction depends on how much authority is acquired from state legislatures or reserved by Congress when a state is created. The report classifies the legislative jurisdiction as 1) exclusive legislative jurisdiction, 2) concurrent legislative jurisdiction (shared with states), 3) partial legislative jurisdiction, and 4) proprietary interest only. [123] All four of these degrees of U.S. legislative authority are based on federal ownership of land within the states.

"Areas over which the Federal Government has acquired exclusive legislative jurisdiction are subject to the exclusive criminal jurisdiction of the United States," states the *Report*. [124] Congress exercises its exclusive plenary criminal jurisdiction in these areas defined by 18 USC 7. "(T)he transfer to the United States of exclusive legislative jurisdiction over an area has the effect, speaking generally, of divesting the State and any governmental entities operating under its authority...," reads the *Report*. [125]

That the states can neither define nor make punishment for crimes in such federal areas is made clear in the case of *In re Ladd* (1896). There the federal court wrote: "the state certainly cannot claim jurisdiction criminally by reason of acts done at places beyond, or not within, its territorial jurisdiction." [126]

Thus, in review, we have seen three normal circumstances when the U.S. government has criminal jurisdiction within the states: 1) when a criminal commits a federal enumerated crime such as counterfeiting, 2) when a criminal commits an offense against the United States, such as bombing a federal building, and 3) when the U.S. government has reserved or been granted exclusive or concurrent criminal jurisdiction over federal lands within the states.

As mentioned, there is a fourth circumstance when Congress gains criminal authority within a state. This may occur when the U.S. Constitution is amended. For example, the 18th Amendment, which prohibited the commerce of alcohol, granted concurrent criminal jurisdiction between Congress and the states over alcohol commerce within the states.

Otherwise and normally, absent such an amendment, states and Congress exercise concurrent regulatory power over all interstate commerce, but neither the states nor Congress can exercise any criminal power over commerce.

Likewise, absent such an amendment or absent concurrent jurisdiction within the federal areas, which would be immortalized by statutory law, then the states and Congress do not share any criminal authority. Very rarely, such as in the Oklahoma City bombing tragedy, may both a state and a U.S. court rightly claim criminal jurisdiction over the same incident.

Thus, 1) states and Congress share the police power of regulation, where Congress' regulatory power is supreme over that of states, and 2) notwithstanding the four exceptions noted above, states have exclusive jurisdiction over crime within their borders. The U.S. Supreme Court explained this in *Caha v. United States* (1894):

"Generally speaking, within any state of this Union the preservation of the peace and the protection of person and property are the functions of the state government, and are not part of the primary duty, at least, of the nation. The laws of Congress in respect to those matters do not extend into the territorial limits of the states, but have force only in the District of Columbia, and other places that are within the exclusive jurisdiction of the national government." [127]

"Those matters" referred to by the Court in *Caha v. United States* (1894) are regulatory and criminal matters that invoke the exercise of republics' two police powers. As we have seen, Congress has regulatory authority within the states based on the Interstate Commerce clause and the Naturalization clause. [128]

However, the laws of Congress in respect to criminal matters normally "do not extend into the territorial limits of the states," wrote the Court in *Caha*, "but have force only in the District of Columbia, and other places that are within the

133

exclusive jurisdiction of the national government." [129]

These "laws of Congress" include most of the criminal provisions in the U.S. Criminal Code, which is Title 18 of the United States Code. The bulk of these statutes, including Congress' criminal prohibitions against guns and drugs, operate solely within the federal areas.

Due to the territorial nature of legislative jurisdiction, then criminal jurisdiction is, with the few exceptions noted above, the exclusive province of states. In other words, says the *Report:*

> "while the Federal Government has power under various provisions of the constitution to define, and prohibit as criminal, certain acts or omissions occurring anywhere in the United States [i.e., crimes relating to federal functions and offenses against the United States, discussed above], it has no power to punish for various other crimes, jurisdiction over which is retained by the States under our Federal-State system of government unless such crimes occur on areas as to which legislative jurisdiction has been vested in the Federal Government," [i.e., the federal areas and enclaves]. [130]

Whether Congress' legislation applies only to the federal areas, or whether it is republican and applies to the fifty states, is strictly a question of legislative jurisdiction (power). As the U.S. Supreme Court wrote in *Cohens v. Virginia* (1821):

> "Whether any particular law be designed to operate without the District or not, depends on the words of that law.. In such cases the constitution and the law must be compared and construed. This is the exercise of jurisdiction. It is the only exercise of it which is allowed in such a case." [131]

In *United States v. Fox* (1877) the U.S. Supreme Court wrote that it is a state crime when "an act committed in a state has no relation to the execution of a power of Congress or to any matter within the jurisdiction of the United States." [132] In other words, it is a state crime when the action is not an offense against the United States, when it is not related to a federal enumerated power, or when it is not committed within the territorial jurisdiction of Congress, as defined at 18 USC 7.

This is what the U.S. Supreme Court told us in *Bond v. United States* (2014):

"In our federal system, the National Government posesses only limited powers; the States and the people retain the remainder. The States have broad authority to enact legislation for the public good – what we have often called a 'police power.' *United States v. Lopez*, 514 U.S. 549, 567 (1995). The Federal Government, by contrast, has no such authority and "can exercise only the powers granted to it," *McCulloch v. Maryland*, 4 Wheat. 316, 405 (1819), including the power to make 'all Laws which shall be necessary and proper for carrying into Execution' the enumerated powers, U.S. Const., Art. I, § 8, cl. 18. For nearly two centuries it has been 'clear' that, lacking a police power, 'Congress cannot punish felonies generally.' *Cohens v. Virginia*, 6 Wheat. 264 (1821). A criminal act committed wholly within a State 'cannot be made an offence against the United States, unless it have some relation to the execution of a power of Congress, or to some matter within the jurisdiction of the United States.' *United States v. Fox*, 95 U.S. 670, 672 (1878)." [133]

Thus, while Congress is the supreme sovereign regulator over interstate commerce and over foreigners within the United States, most crimes committed within the states are state crimes, subject to state prosecutions. In fact, there are relatively few federal crimes within the states to be adjudicated by Article III judicial courts.

In conclusion, these past two sections have been about how Congress legislates as a republic with regard to the state republics. As a republic, Congress exercises two police powers, i.e., regulation and criminal prohibition, just like the states do. As a republic, Congress is required to use the same natural law definitions of case, crime and commerce that the states as republics must use.

Congress' regulatory power is supreme over that of the states. However, with only the four exceptions noted above, and reiterated by the U.S. Supreme Court in *Bond v. United States* (2014), states generally have supreme jurisdiction over crimes committed within their borders.

Thus, one of the pillars of federalism has now been defined, i.e., how the states and Congress – each as republics – share their two police powers of regulation and criminal prohibition, respectively under equity and law.

Federalism, part 2: Congress' two legislative capacities

Within America's republics, the U.S. Constitution requires that states and Congress have the above-outlined relationship, and that they share the same definition of case and crime.

However, in contrast to the Congress that legislates as a republic with regard to the states, this section explains how Congress also legislates as a nonrepublic in the federal areas, outside of state authority. In these areas, Congress is not required to operate as a republic, with its guarantees of due process and its separations of power.

As mentioned earlier, this means that – depending upon where one is – then one is not always guaranteed a republican form of government in the United States. Thus, one is not always guaranteed all of the protections under the Bill of Rights.

In such areas or circumstances, including on all navigable U.S. waterways and in ships and airliners registered to the United States, Congress legislates as a nonrepublic. There, the limitations upon positive law that are imposed by natural law within sovereign republics are not recognized, and all political rights are bestowed by Congress, and none by nature.

To best understand how Congress legislates as a nonrepublic over the federal areas, let us review some features of the nonrepublican form of government. As we shall see, the legal characteristics of nonrepublics, which are summarized below, are some of those same features that U.S. courts, including the U.S. Supreme Court, attribute to Congress' power within the federal areas:

1. that nonrepublics have unnatural power to subjectively define judicial cases and crimes without reference to objective natural law, which means that torts and crimes are *malum prohibita*, or whatever the monarch, oligarch or majority say they are,

2. that nonrepublics enforce their subjective beliefs and opinions with plenary power over artificial persons, and that their courts exercise no law jurisdiction, where natural law can be enforced and where natural people's natural political rights can be secured from lawmakers,

3. that a nonrepublic's subjects a) are not natural born, but are born subject to an artificial sovereign, without natural rights, and b) are not free of government as a result of being born into subjecthood, under claim,

4. that there exists no separation of power between branches of government in a nonrepublic, all of which serve the sole sovereign,

5. that all the political "rights" are in fact legal privileges and immunities that the sovereign has granted to its subjects, and are not inherited natural rights, and

6. that the nonrepublic's artificial authority comes not from the natural delegation of power from citizens, but instead from the artificial claim of power by the lawmaker, based on the use of force and fraud, be it a divine appointment from God or a false claim of natural power.

Given these characteristics of a nonrepublican form of government, there are at least four provisions in the U.S. Constitution that support the view that Congress may legislate as a nonrepublic in the federal areas.

The first thing to note is that the U.S. Constitution did not make the District of Columbia and other federal areas a state to which the Guaranty Clause applies. Article IV, Section 4 of the U.S. Constitution guarantees "to every State in this Union a Republican Form of Government." Because the federal areas are not a state, then Congress is not explicitly required to guarantee a republican form of government within those areas.

A second argument is that the 13th Amendment's prohibition against slavery does not appear to apply in the federal areas. This would suggest that Congress can enslave people there without the commission of a *malum in se* crime, such as in matters of disfavored drug and gun commerce.

Arguably the 13th Amendment does not apply to the federal areas because it prohibits slavery only "within the United States, or any place subject to their jurisdiction." Not only are the federal areas not subject to state jurisdiction, but slavery can only exist in a nonrepublic 1) which does not respect natural law, and 2) which is not required to provide a law jurisdiction where due process of law is available to all natural persons.

A third argument is that Article I, Section 8, Clause 17 of

138

the U.S. Constitution, which grants Congress "exclusive Legislation in all Cases whatsoever," means that Congress can legislate the meaning of "all Cases whatsoever" within the federal area. This would mean that it could legislate the meaning of criminal cases, irrespective of how natural law defines case, controversy, crime and probable cause within America's republics.

A fourth argument is that Congress legislates over people within the federal areas as subjects, often called citizen-subjects, instead of toward them as republican citizens. This is the mark of a nonrepublic. Republics answer to their citizens, whereas subjects answer to the nonrepublics that created them.

The 14th Amendment refers to "(a)ll persons born or naturalized in the United States and <u>subject</u> to the jurisdiction thereof." This does not describe, and is in contrast to, natural born Citizens 1) who gain their citizenship through the political act of their citizen fathers, outside of Congress' authority, 2) who need not be born or naturalized in the United States to be citizens, and 3) who are not born subject to or subjects of the equity jurisdiction of the U.S. government.

That the 14th Amendment requires only states to provide due process of law and equal protection to all persons, and not Congress, is compatible with this analysis of Congress' powers.

These are solid arguments that the constitution allows Congress to legislate as a nonrepublic within the federal areas, where it can define crime – and enslave people – without regard to natural law and the Bill of Rights.

This would allow Congress to violate people's natural right to liberty there, and for Congress to deprive select merchants of administrative due process for engaging in certain unwanted commerce. As well, because inhabitants of Washington, D.C. and other federal areas have a subject-status, it is hard to deny that they live under a nonrepublic.

Because of these reasons, and because the federal areas need a municipal court system just as the states do, the U.S. Constitution provides for and circumstances require Congress to establish its own court system for the federal areas and certain federal functions.

These courts are called Article I courts (or legislative courts) because they are created by Congress based on its legislative powers that are granted under Article I of the U.S. Constitution. These are contrasted with U.S. judicial courts – called Article III courts – that are created under authority of Article III of the U.S. Constitution, to which the Case or Controversy requirement applies. [134]

Article III courts operate within America's state republics. They adjudicate only cases, which by definition involve an injury to a right. Article I courts operate only over the federal areas and over certain federal functions.

These Article I courts include territorial courts (as in the district of Guam, the U.S. Virgin Islands and the Northern Mariana Islands), the U.S. Court of Military Appeals, the U.S. Court of Veterans Appeals, the U.S. Court of Federal Claims and the U.S. Tax Court, for instance.

Whereas Article III courts adjudicate violations of natural rights, commercial conflicts, federal crimes and federal questions on behalf of the U.S. republic, Article I courts enforce Congress' plenary authority in the federal areas. This includes adjudicating the privileges and immunities that Congress grants to the people who are subject to its jurisdiction there.

This means that Article I judges are administrators for the federal areas and enforcers of Congress' absolute powers. Without a natural jurisdiction, they administer the will of Congress instead of providing republican justice for the people.

They are "not members of the independent judiciary which has been one of our proudest boasts, by reason of Art. III," wrote Justice William Douglas of the U.S. Supreme Court in his dissent in *Palmore v. United States* (1973). [135] This is to say that they are not judicial officers who administer the law jurisdiction where, for example, natural rights are secured.

Note that what the U.S. Supreme Court and other courts say (below) about Congress' power over the District of Columbia is also applicable to Congress' power in the other federal areas. At 18 USC 7, Congress makes no distinctions between the District of Columbia and the other federal areas.

The constitution "confers upon Congress the power to establish courts within the District of Columbia and to define the extent of the jurisdiction of such courts," wrote the Massachusetts District Court in *Ostrow v. Samuel Brilliant Co.* (1946). [136] This power includes the "authority to vest courts of the District of Columbia with a variety of jurisdiction," wrote the Court of Appeals for the District of Columbia in *Hill v. Dorsey* (1927). [137] Congress "may, if it sees fit, unite legislative and judicial powers in a single hand," wrote the *Hill v. Dorsey* court citing *Keller v. Potomac Electric Company* (1922) [138]

This plenary power to create Article I courts and to vest them with a variety of muddled power is in contrast with Congress' lack of authority to change the jurisdiction of Article III courts, whose jurisdiction is constitutionally fixed by the Case or Controversy Requirement. As well, whereas Article III courts respect the separation of powers between the executive. legislative and judicial branches of government, Article I courts can unite them "in a single hand." [139]

"Congress has the entire control over the district for every purpose of government, and it is reasonable to suppose that in organizing a judicial department in this District, all the judicial power necessary for the purposes of government would be vested in the courts of justice," the U.S. Supreme Court wrote in *Kendall v. United States* (1838). [140]

This plenary power to create its own courts and to define the extent of their jurisdiction are extraordinary powers that Congress may not exercise over Article III courts. This is because such Article III courts owe their existence – not to

Congress – but to the U.S. Constitution.

Thus, Congress controls the jurisdiction of Article I courts, but it does not control the jurisdiction of Article III courts. This is a separation of power. With regard to Article III courts, it must legislate consistently with their republican jurisdiction, based on injury, pursuant to the U.S. Constitution.

Likewise, state judicial courts owe their existence to state constitutions, not to state legislatures. That is why constitutional amendments are required to change or expand the powers of state and federal judicial courts.

The power of Congress is plenary in the District of Columbia, wrote Justice Douglas in *Palmore v. United States* (1973), when it gives "Congress authority to establish the method by which the District of Columbia will be governed, and to alter from time to time the form of that government." [141]

As we seen from the beginning, there are only two forms of government, i.e., republics and nonrepublics. Thus, to be able "to alter from time to time the form of that government" is extraordinary legislative power that is not found in America's republics or in Congress legislating with regard to them.

"In exercising this power, Congress is not subject to the same constitutional limitations, as when it is legislating for the United States..." wrote the U.S. Supreme Court in *Hooven & Allison Co. v. Evatt* (1945). [142]

> "And in general the guaranties of the constitution, save as they are limitations upon the exercise of executive and legislative power when exerted for or over our insular possessions, extend to them only as Congress, in the exercise of its legislative power over territory belonging to the United States, has made those guaranties applicable." [143]

In other words, Congress has constitutional limitations when legislating as a republic for the union of state republics, a) where for example it regulates commerce and foreigners, b) where natural law defines crime, and c) where injury defines judicial jurisdiction. However, the guarantees of the U.S. Constitution that extend to the federal areas or to the people in them are only as Congress "has made those guarantees applicable." [144]

Thus, according to the U.S. Supreme Court, Congress has exclusive authority in the federal areas to determine what rights – both substantive and natural rights – apply. Apparently as well, both Congress and its Article I courts may disregard the natural law, the constitutional definition of crime, the Case or Controversy requirement, [145] the Due Process clauses, [146] the Equal Protection clause, [147] and other guarantees of republican government, and may instead determine which rights apply.

The power to determine what rights are applicable – instead of acknowledging that rights come naturally – is what makes governments nonrepublican. This is because non-republics do not recognize the law jurisdiction of republican judicial courts a) where crime is objectively defined by natural law to include injury, b) where natural law defines primary citizenship, and c) where natural rights are unalienable and not subject to legislative opinion.

The U.S. Supreme Court in *Palmore v. United States* (1973) echoed the sentiments of *Hooven* (1945). "It is apparent," wrote the *Palmore* Court, "that the power of Congress under Clause 17 permits it to legislate for the District in a manner with respect to subjects that would exceed its powers, or at least would be very unusual, in the context of national legislation enacted under other powers delegated to it under Art. I, § 8." [148]

Given that Congress must legislate toward the states as a republic, this would make the "national legislation" referred to in the above quotation to mean: republican legislation. Thus, the courts conclude that the plenary (unlimited) powers that Congress exercises in the federal areas exceed those limited powers that it may exercise as a republic among the states.

As well, as pointed out by the *Palmore* majority, such authority in the federal areas is exercised "with respects to subjects" [149] – meaning with respect to subjects of a nonrepublic – rather than with respect to republican citizens. A nonrepublic does not recognize the natural political rights of citizens, but instead only the artificial "rights" that the sovereign bestows upon its subjects or citizen-subjects.

Nonrepublics have no basis in nature. They and natural law are antithetical, incompatible and cannot operate in the same space. This is because nonrepublican sovereigns claim unnatural power, for example the power to define everyone else's political rights unequally. That describes the power that Congress exercises within the federal areas.

Thus, as the above *Hooven* (1945) and *Palmore* (1973) cases tell us, the criminal and civil jurisdictions of Article I courts are as Congress determines, and their criminal jurisdiction may be enlarged over that subject matter which state judicial courts and Article III courts have authority to adjudicate, which is injury to a right.

This leads to the conclusion that Congress' Article I courts may adjudicate matters that do not include injury, and that these courts are not subject to the Case or Controversy requirement to which Article III courts are subject.

If this analysis is correct, then Congress is adjudged a nonrepublic in the federal areas, where it may criminally prohibit *malum prohibita* in its Article I courts. This is because Congress has authority to define both crime and probable cause for its artificial subjects within the federal areas.

This means that Congress, which the *Hooven* (1945) court said could determine which rights are applicable in the federal areas, may deny the right of property possession and administrative due process, and may criminalize *malum prohibita* within its legislative Article I courts, which it may not do in Article III courts that operate within the states.

Congress has constitutional power, wrote the *Palmore*

144

(1972) Court, "to proscribe certain criminal conduct only in the District and to select the appropriate court, whether it is created by virtue of article III or article I, to hear and determine these particular criminal cases within the District." [150]

This quotation signifies two additional reasons that Congress' rule in the federal areas is nonrepublican. First, to proscribe (prohibit) certain criminal conduct only in the federal areas is in direct contrast with the lack of this power in American republics, where nature proscribes crime and legislatures merely prescribe it.

Second, that Congress can decide to adjudicate crime in either Article III or Article I courts means that crimes in the federal areas are not always subject to the republican criteria of Article III courts, i.e., injury. Suggested the *Palmore* Court, Congress may try *malum in se* that occurs within the federal areas in Article III courts and may criminally prosecute its *malum prohibita* in Article I courts, where cases or controversies are not required. [151]

Article I courts "handle criminal cases only under statutes that are applicable to the District of Columbia alone," wrote the U.S. Supreme Court in *Palmore*. [152] This is because nonrepublican criminal statutes would not be enforceable within the states, where all cases require proof of injury.

Thus, based on the above various case law, we can see that the exercise of Congress in the federal areas is nonrepublican. This is 1) because its Article I courts do not have a Case or Controversy requirement for criminal prosecutions, [153] 2) because there is no separation of powers between branches of government (because the police powers serve Congress as the nonrepublic, not the people), 3) because Congress can divvy-out rights as it chooses (as if it is a monarch, above nature), 4) because Congress can enslave people without the commission of crimes (because the 13th Amendment, the law jurisdiction and due process of law do not necessarily apply in the federal areas), and 5) because federal visitors, inhabitants and U.S. citizens

145

serve Congress as subjects there.

Only this nonrepublican form of government accounts for the criminal prohibitions in the U.S. Criminal Code against such things as unwanted drugs and guns. Within the republican states, where Congress regulates commerce and where it has very limited criminal jurisdiction, Congress has no criminal jurisdiction over drug or gun commerce.

None of this subject matter fits under the four exceptions to exclusive state criminal jurisdiction. Thus, the judicial authority for prosecuting these false criminal prohibitions within the states is based on pure opinion, and not fact.

Congress can criminalize *malum prohibita* only in the federal areas 1) where it is sovereign with the power of "exclusive Legislation" [154] and 2) where it may legislate as a nonrepublic, without regard to the natural law definitions of crime or the subject matter jurisdiction of Article III judicial courts.

In fact, as a nonrepublic in the federal areas, Congress can redefine such naturally-defined things as case, crime, citizen, mother, father, family, male, female and marriage in any manner it wishes. Outside of Congress' guarantee to the states of a republican form of government, Congress is not bound in the federal areas by what is natural, objective and verifiable.

Examples of Congress' two legislative capacities

As we have seen in the last few sections, Congress legislates in two capacities. First, it legislates as would a republic with regard to the states, wherein it regulates interstate commerce and has very little criminal authority. Second, it legislates as would a nonrepublic with regard to the federal areas, wherein it – instead of nature – grants everyone their political rights. These two legislative capacities can be discerned not only from the U.S. Constitution and federal case law, as we discussed above, but also from Congress' statutes regarding at least guns, drugs and income taxes.

146

Take for example 21 USC 841(a) which makes it a crime "to manufacture, distribute, or dispense, or possess with intent to manufacture, distribute, or dispense, a controlled substance."

Compare this with 21 USC 822(a), which says that every person who manufactures, distributes or dispenses controlled substances, or who proposes to do this, must "obtain annually a registration issued by the Attorney General in accordance with the rules and regulations promulgated by him..." [155] Both provisions are from the same U.S. Controlled Substances Act.

These provisions appear to be in direct conflict. One criminally prohibits drug commerce, while the other regulates it through licensing. If the statutes are taken together and out of context, then the Attorney General appears to be able to license crime. Such conflicts could render the U.S. Controlled Substances Act unconstitutional.

However, these provisions are neither in conflict nor unconstitutional because they operate in separate territorial jurisdictions. The criminal prohibition against unwanted drug dealing at 21 USC 841(a) is applicable in the federal areas. The regulatory provisions at 21 USC 822 apply to drug dealing within and between the state republics. [156]

Congress' two legislative capacities are also evident in U.S. gun statutes. 18 USC 922 criminalizes gun dealing in the federal areas, while 18 USC 923 requires gun dealers within the fifty states to be licensed by the Attorney General.

This same dichotomy goes for one's failure to file an income tax form, which is a regulatory violation within America's republics. Nonetheless Willful Failure to File an income tax form is criminalized at 26 USC 7203. Based upon the meaning of crime within a republic, this prohibition can only apply in the federal areas, subject to Congress' nonrepublican authority.

Also note that the above drug, gun and tax "crimes" are only crimes in Article I courts. However, for half a century or more these "crimes" have been falsely litigated throughout the United States in Article III courts.

147

This false, frivolous and unlawful litigation is the result of attorneys not knowing 1) that Congress legislates over two separate territorial areas, i.e., the fifty states and the federal areas, and respectively in two different manners, i.e., republican and nonrepublican, 2) that Congress' can criminalize regulatory omissions and other non-crimes only in the federal areas, and 3) that Congress regulates all commerce within the states.

Therefore to read any U.S. legislation properly, it is necessary to know in which sovereign capacity that Congress created the legislation. This capacity is evident by the police power, i.e., criminal prohibition or regulation, which Congress applies to particular behavior.

If Congress' treatment is regulatory, then the provision applies where Congress may regulate commerce and aliens, i.e., in every square inch of the United States. However, if a provision is prohibitory, and does not regard a federal enumerated crime or an offense against the Untied States, then it necessarily applies in the federal areas where Congress – and not nature – determines the criteria for incarceration.

Thus, we know that the regulatory provisions at 21 USC 822 and 18 USC 923 apply within America's republics, and that the criminal prohibitory provisions at 21 USC 841(a), 18 USC 922 and 26 USC 7203 apply only within the federal areas.

As we have learned, Article III courts have no subject matter jurisdiction over *malum prohibita* within the states. Their jurisdiction is over injury to a right. Within America's states – outside the federal areas – *malum prohibita* is enforced primarily in the executive branch by regulators using the equitable powers of forfeiture, injunction and specific performance.

With this knowledge, we can see that the criminal prosecutions of drug, gun and tax offenses that apply in the federal areas are independent of the U.S. Attorney General's power to regulate drug, gun and taxable commerce among the states.

This knowledge is necessary in order to properly read the United States criminal code at Title 18 USC. This knowledge allows the reader to see that this "criminal code" contains not only prohibitory criminal provisions, but also regulatory provisions. As we have seen, Title 18 both prohibits and regulates gun commerce, but in separate places within the country.

As well, this knowledge allows the reader to discern 1) crimes legislated under Congress' enumerated authority and applicable within the states, such counterfeiting and forgery (see Title 18, Chapter 25), from 2) crimes legislated for the federal areas, such as drug, gun and tax offenses, which occur under Congress' plenary (aboslute) authority at Article I, Section 8, Clause 17 of the U.S. Constitution.

U.S. republican law treats the commerce of drugs, tobacco, alcohol, chemicals and guns fundamentally the same. It regulates their commerce. This is because each are forms of property, and because the commerce of property operates in equity – not under criminal law.

Thus, one must know *a priori* the respective powers of the U.S. republic and of the U.S. nonrepublic, as well as those of law and equity, to discern where the provisions of Title 18 (the U.S. criminal code), Title 21 (which includes the U.S. Controlled Substances Act) and Title 26 (the Internal Revenue Code) apply. One must know *a priori* the differences between Congress as the U.S. republic and Congress as a nonrepublic to properly read all the regulatory and criminal statutes in the United States Code.

The criminal prosecutions in Article III and state judicial courts of people for drug and gun dealing, which are regulatory violations within the state republics, are evidence that most American criminal attorneys have not known the differences.

The separation of admiralty from the law of the land

We discussed that there are two judicial jurisdictions that operate in America's republics: law and equity. However, there is a third judicial power mentioned in Article III of the U.S. Constitution. It is called admiralty or maritime.

Black's Law Dictionary says that "(t)he terms 'admiralty' and ' maritime' law are virtually synonymous." [157] They pertain "to navigable waters, i.e., to the sea, ocean, great lakes, navigable rivers, or the navigation or commerce thereof." [158]

As we have seen, these navigable waters are a part of the federals areas, defined at 18 USC 7, which are subject solely to Congress' nonrepublican rule. Says *Black's Law Dictionary*, maritime law is "(t)hat which the Congress has enacted or the Federal courts, sitting in admiralty, or in the exercise of their maritime jurisdiction, have declared and would apply." [159]

Thus, Congress is the sole sovereign over America's navigable waters, able to create and declare nonrepublican law there. People's rights that apply in the federal areas are what Congress and its courts "have declared and would apply..." [160]

This is exactly the same congressional power as the Supreme Court described for all the federal areas in *Hooven & Allison v. Evatt* (1945) – i.e., that all rights that exist there are what Congress makes applicable. [161]

Thus, Congress rules federal land, navigable waterways and air transportation – which make up the federal areas – essentially the same. Rights there are as Congress declares.

In contrast, natural and substantive rights under the Bill of Rights are guaranteed by the U.S. Constitution only in the territorial areas of the fifty states where the states and Congress must operate as republics. This includes states' non-navigable lakes, streams and rivers.

This means that if a crime is committed, for instance on a boat on the Ohio River – which is navigable – then it is a U.S. crime, subject to Congress' criminal code for the federal areas. But if a crime is committed on a landlocked lake within Ohio, then it is an Ohio crime. This is due solely to the separation of territorial criminal jurisdiction between the state of Ohio and the nonrepublican Congress, whose river and criminal jurisdiction border southern Ohio.

Perhaps the reader has heard of the term "the law of the

land." *Black's Law Dictionary* accurately and succinctly defines it as "due process of law." [162]

As we have seen, due process of law is a substantive right that is owed by federal and state courts to all natural persons within the law jurisdiction of state republics. It is not that process which applies to artificial persons in the federal areas – operating in equity or admiralty – which is whatever administrative or criminal process that Congress makes applicable.

The law jurisdiction and its due process of law do not apply to artificial persons in the federal areas. They do not apply in Congress' Article I courts in the federal areas, which adjudicate the privileges and immunities of Congress' subjects.

So, the law of the land, or due process of law, is that owed to all natural persons within America's republics, outside of the federal areas. This republican law of the land is opposite and opposed to the nonrepublican law of the federal areas, including that on its navigable waters.

These federal areas are where Congress need not respect natural rights of individuals, where it may prohibit – instead of just regulate – commerce, and where the Bill of Rights and due process of law are not applicable unless Congress says so.

This is because due process of law is mandatory only in the law jurisdiction of state and Article III judicial courts which enforce natural criminal law. This is the only jurisdiction where the natural rights of natural persons are recognized.

In the (natural) law jurisdiction, nature defines one's rights, not Man. Thus, due process of law is not subject to Man, as is the law of the federal areas.

Congress is not required to recognize or secure due process of law and the natural law jurisdiction in the federal areas – whether on land, on water or on ships and airplanes registered to the United States. In these areas, there are no recognized natural rights because everyone entering these areas explicitly or tacitly consent to be governed by Congress as artificial persons.

As artificial persons, in the absence of a judicial law jurisdiction, then people are owed merely what Congress grants to them under its plenary capacity. Natural right and wrong are not adjudged in this jurisdiction, but only the artificial standards of the territorial sovereign. Whether operating out of equity or admiralty, Congress has plenary power over both jurisdictions within the federal areas.

In these areas, a) where Congress determines which rights are applicable, b) where there is no separation of power between government branches, and c) where all power is exercised on behalf of Congress as the sole sovereign, then there is little if any difference between equity and admiralty law, except that one operates on soil and the other on water.

So, whether on federal land, on navigable waters or in airplanes registered to the U.S. government, all persons there are artificial, and everyone and everything is subject to Congress as they would be to a captain on a ship. There, equity and admiralty mean whatever Congress says they mean, and they mean essentially the same thing.

Thus, we can figuratively characterize all law of the nonrepublican Congress in the federal areas as the law of the sea. This is contrasted to republican law within the states, where due process of law is required, which is the law of the land. Nonrepublics enforce the criminal law of the sole sovereign, whether it be a captain, dictator or legislature. In contrast, republics enforce the criminal law of nature, based on the objective standard of injury.

Due process of law, or the law of the land, is what America's republics owe to natural persons. It serves only to secure the natural law authority of individuals. It does not serve positive law in any manner. Instead, positive law serves it.

Given this, I present here an anomaly for readers to consider and resolve. I mentioned earlier that the provision in Arizona Senate Bill 1070, which criminalized the failure of foreigners to carry their state registration papers, was declared invalid because of the Supremacy Clause.

This is because there is a like provision in the Immigration and Naturalization Act, codified at 8 USC 1304(e), which criminalizes the failure to carry U.S. registration papers. This provision says that it is a misdemeanor for a foreigner to not carry his papers. The Supreme Court said that this U.S. provision preempts the same provision in Arizona's law.

I contend here that this U.S. provision would be unenforceable within the states where nature defines what is criminal – not Congress. As with drug, gun and tax "crimes," this criminal provision can only apply within the federal areas where Congress can criminalize artificial duties. Within the states, these are civil violations, subject to civil – not criminal – penalties.

Within the states, where constitutions define crime as *malum in se* – and where officials can only regulate unwanted foreigners, disfavored businesses and delinquent taxpayers as *malum prohibita* – then none of these regulatory violators are subject to criminal prosecution. Lacking victims, their unwanted behavior is illegal under a legislature's non-criminal equity jurisdiction, but is not unlawful under the criminal law jurisdiction, where judicial power requires an injury to a right.

Each sovereign is a check upon another

At the beginning of this book, we mentioned the idea of plenary power. *Black's Law Dictionary* defines plenary as "full, entire, complete, absolute, perfect, unqualified." [163] Sovereignty is the exercise of plenary power over specific subject matter.

Further into the book we discovered that there are four sovereigns under American law. These are: 1) the fifty state republics, 2) Congress legislating as a republic with regard to these state republics, 3) Congress legislating as a nonrepublic over the federal areas, and 4) individuals exercising their natural rights within the fifty states, and outside of Congress' territorial, subject matter and contractual jurisdictions.

These are sovereigns because they exercise their own

plenary legislative or adjudicative power over their own subject matter. Plenary describes the full extent of each sovereign's authority <u>under</u> the constitution.

Such complete power is always *a priori* limited by the legislative and subject matter jurisdiction of the sovereign. Thus, one cannot understand a sovereign's unqualified power without first understanding the scope of its legislative and adjudicatory authority that constitutions delegate or reserve.

Each sovereign has absolute or plenary authority to exercise its delegated or reserved powers. Such powers can be rightly exercised to the extent that they do not infringe upon the scope of another sovereign's powers.

For example, Congress has complete power to regulate interstate commerce in equity, but this does not include the power to criminally prohibit commerce at law, for which Congress has no legislative jurisdiction.

Congress also has unqualified authority to legislate over naturalization, and naturalized citizens. However, this power does not include any authority to legislate the meaning of natural born Citizen, which is a natural law term, or to legislate over such natural law citizens within the states.

Likewise, Congress in its nonrepublican capacity has full power to legislate the rights of all artificial persons in the federal areas. However, it lacks authority there to determine the political rights of the President and Vice President. This is for several self-evident reasons.

First, the President and Vice President serve in a natural representative capacity. They are sent to Washington, D.C. because of their natural political rights as natural born Citizens, not in spite of them. Such offices are not bestowed privileges by Congress but the fulfillment of a natural, inherent and unalienable political right by these prominent natural law citizens.

This is also for a practical reason: that if the President and Vice President were subjects of Congress as are all others in the federal areas, then Congress could criminalize their personal behavior in order to silence or jail them.

Thus, the President and Vice President are the only natural born Citizens whose natural rights Congress must fully respect within not only the state republics, where Congress must respect the rights of all natural persons and all natural law citizens, but also within the federal areas as well, where Congress otherwise defines everyone's rights.

This means that the President and Vice President are the only state citizens in the federal areas 1) over whom Congress may not adversely legislate, 2) to whom Congress owes a republican form of government (with its Bill of Rights and due process of law), and 3) who Congress cannot criminalize with its *malum prohibita*, as it does the unwanted behavior of all others.

The President and Vice President are the only U.S. citizens with republican rights in the federal areas. They are the only natural born Citizens who carry the law of the land with them, while everyone else there is subject to the law of the sea.

Such natural law leaders are not subjects of Congress, but are instead co-equals to Congress, as the Separation of Powers Doctrine requires. Thus, Congress' artificial authority over the federal areas is held in check by the natural law authority of the natural representatives of the people. This is yet another example of how positive law is governed by natural law, and this occurs even in the nonrepublican federal areas.

In addition to its powers in the federal areas, Congress also has plenary authority over certain federal crimes within the states. Otherwise the federal government has very limited criminal jurisdiction within the state republics. As well, judicial courts have absolute authority over cases and crimes, but no such subject matter jurisdiction over regulatory matters.

Instead, executive branch agencies have the complete power to regulate. However, this unqualified power to regulate does not include criminal prohibition. This is because regulation in the executive branch is constitutionally held in check by the criminal law jurisdiction of the judicial branch, which holds all of the prohibitory power of America's republics.

As we have seen, legislatures' ultimate authority is limited by the power granted to them in constitutions. Such authority does not include the power to change or expand the criminal jurisdiction of judicial courts. As we also learned, state legislatures have total authority to legislate over artificial persons in equity, but they have no such authority to legislate crimes, which are instead subject to nature's plenary authority.

Individuals are sovereign over certain things. Crime victims, for example, have absolute criminal jurisdiction in matters of self-defense, and U.S. male citizens have primary jurisdiction over the creation of natural born Citizens. Individuals also legislate over what property that they acquire, as well as when they sleep, eat and excrete, for example, subject to nature.

No other sovereigns have authority over this subject matter. Thus, individual sovereigns – who are answerable only to nature – have "full, entire, complete, absolute, perfect (and) unqualified" [164] authority over self-defense, over the creation of natural citizens, and over all other exercises of their other natural rights. When acting outside of positive law authority, then individuals answer only to natural law.

Therefore, each American sovereign has plenary power over its own legislative and adjudicatory jurisdictions. Republican governance requires keeping these absolute powers separate. Such good and proper governance requires the full knowledge and exercise of these powers by each sovereign within the jurisdictional limits imposed by America's constitutions.

Consequently, plenary power really means a sovereign's complete power to exercise that sovereign's rightful authority. This means that in order to define each sovereign's ultimate power, we must first consult republican constitutions, which grant certain powers to the state and federal political sovereigns, and which reserve certain authority for individual sovereigns. Only then can the entire power of each and all of America's sovereigns be properly understood and recognized.

156

This is to be the object of learning American law. It is the object of this book. As the Supreme Court told us in *Yick Wo v. Hopkins* (1896), law is the proper definition, distribution and limitation of power. To know American law is to know how plenary power is to be distributed.

What we have learned so far

Governments are defined as republican or nonrepublican depending on how they distribute and limit power. How they distribute and limit power is called law. Law is what American law schools are supposed to teach.

We have seen that republics are characterized by natural distributions, separations and limitations of power, and that nonrepublics are not. Republics' separations are natural 1) because they recognize the reserved natural powers of individuals, who have not granted government authority over their natural endeavors, and 2) because they are logical and based on natural and objective criteria, and not upon the illogic, subjectivity and opinions of Man.

Justice in republics is based on natural and objective definitions of certain things, such as case, crime, natural born Citizen, and production, which are facts of nature. In contrast, in nonrepublics, these words are always subject to definition by the artificial and inherently whimsical political sovereign.

In such nonrepublics, the sole political sovereign determines who belongs in jail, what the privileges of citizenship are, and what people may produce for themselves. Lacking objective and natural criteria, justice in nonrepublics is by definition artificial, subjective and arbitrary.

This is justice based on Man's law as opposed to the immutable political laws of nature. It is justice based on belief and opinion rather than on objectivity and science.

As we have seen, there are various differences between republican and nonrepublican law. One distinction is that natural law defines certain legal principles in a republic, whereas the role of natural law is denied in the nonrepublican form of government.

Another difference is that in a nonrepublic, there is no separation or limitation of the political sovereign's power, except to the extent that this sovereign has voluntarily agreed to relinquish such unnaturally acquired power.

In contrast, republican law tempers positive law by excluding its authority over certain subject matter. This certain subject matter is natural persons' exercise of natural rights. This separation of power does not exist in nonrepublics which by definition deny the role of nature in law, and where all people and parts of government serve the political sovereign.

Nor does the separation of power between regulation and prohibition exist in a nonrepublic. Because nonrepublics do not define crime objectively, i.e., based on injury to a victim, then the political sovereign can prohibit and regulate what it wishes and how it wishes. In contrast, in an American republic, all commerce is regulated, while only that behavior which is inherently wrong, i.e., *malum in se*, is criminally prohibited.

This is necessitated by a separation of law and equity in America's republics. The law jurisdiction is that judicial authority over breaches of natural law by natural persons.

Because nonrepublics do not acknowledge natural law, then they do not have a judicial jurisdiction that respects the natural rights of their subjects. Subjects' rights are only those that the sovereign makes applicable or has agreed to respect.

In America's federated form of republican government, power is separated on various levels. Within the land areas of the fifty American states, 1) both the U.S. and state governments regulate commerce and foreigners, with the regulatory authority of the U.S. being superior, 2) both the U.S. and state governments define crime as *malum in se*, and 3) states have jurisdiction over crimes within their borders with the four exceptions: a) of federal enumerated crimes, b) of offenses against the United States, c) of crimes within the federal areas, and d) of concurrent crimes based on constitutional amendments. This paragraph succinctly outlines one pillar of federalism, which is how power is shared between the republican Congress and state republican sovereigns.

Under this federalism, slavery is still allowed in the federal areas, where Congress can prohibit anything and arrest anyone, excluding the President and Vice President. The 13th Amendment prohibits slavery only within the states.

This is because the states are republics where the law jurisdiction respects the equality of all natural persons, who are owed due process of law, which is the law of the land. As we have seen, this is not the case in the federal areas where Congress operates essentially as a captain, under the law of the sea.

In the federal areas, Congress defines everyone's rights. Because Congress can deny one the right to liberty, then everyone – except the President and Vice President – is potentially a slave in the nonrepublican federal areas.

Last, what this and my previous book [165] uniquely reveal is that Congress legislates as a nonrepublic with respect to the federal areas, and that its nonrepublican legislation over such areas does not apply within the states. Within the states, the United States shares regulatory power with these republics and has limited criminal powers within them.

More importantly, these books show that criminal legislation that is intended by Congress for the federal areas and for Article I courts is being falsely enforced within the state republics in Article III courts. This is analogous to the states' false enforcement of regulatory matters in their judicial courts. This evidences a fundamental failure in the republican form of government's various separations of power.

Ignorance of the law does not excuse [166]

This book has defined America's federated republican

form of government and its sharing of power between four sovereigns, each with their own rightful constitutional authority. Federalism is the definition of power between American states and Congress in the various above-described manners.

But this accurate description does not accurately describe how American law – as a product of American attorneys – in fact operates. For example, take the judicially waged war on drugs. It violates the Separation of Powers Doctrine (judicial courts doing the work of regulatory courts), the 13th Amendment (non-criminals being enslaved), and the Equal Protection Clause (unequal treatment for disfavored manufacturers, distributors and dispensers of controlled substances).

As we have seen, American law says 1) that drug (property) possession is a natural right in America's republics, 2) that drug commerce is subject to regulation in the executive branch under equity, and 3) that criminal drug prohibition operates only in the federal areas, enforced in Article I courts.

However, in spite of this law and all the statutes that support it, both drug possession and drug dealing are tried as crimes in state and U.S. judicial courts, which have criminal jurisdiction only over cases involving injury-in-fact.

The reason for this false enforcement of law is that knowledge about America's republican form of government does not exist within the legal community. That is, the essential information in this book about the natural law basis of the U.S. Constitution and about various separations of power is not known by American attorneys, all ironically who take oaths to uphold the U.S. Constitution and its republican form of government.

Although the U.S. Constitution guarantees to the states a republican form of government, this guarantee is not readily discussed in law schools. In fact, illustrative of its lack of importance in legal education, Cornell University Law School promulgates the view at its website that "(n)o one can now resurrect the full meaning of the (Guarantee) clause and intent which moved the Framers to adopt it." [167]

This statement is patently absurd 1) because this book resurrects the meaning of the Guaranty Clause at Article IV, Section 4, 2) because the intent of the clause is clear, i.e., that Congress will legislate consistently with the republican form of government of the states, within the states, and 3) because "the full meaning of the clause" is apparent to anyone who knows the meaning of a republic, which "supposes a form already established" [168] that is therefore inherent, discernible and knowable.

As we have seen, the meaning of the republican form of government is essentially self-evident. However, its various essential separations of power can be elusive until one sees the role of natural law, and its separation from positive law. I first saw this separation when I learned that there are natural law citizens (called natural born Citizens) and positive law citizens (called Citizens of the United States).

That natural law defines natural born Citizens indicated to me that there is both a natural and positive law jurisdiction in the U.S. Constitution. From this I surmised that natural law defines other important law terms, which are also not subject to legislatures. Given these pillars of knowledge, and based on my formal education and former law practice, then just about everything else that I relate in this book – which is mostly about republics' various separations of powers – fell into logical order.

This is to say that most other attorneys are equally equipped to understand the republic form of government, and their personal obligations under the U.S. Constitution, if provided a few missing pieces to the puzzle, which this book provides. The biggest piece that is missing from American law-school education is that natural law is the basis of the U.S. Constitution, which serves to hold positive law in check. This dual sovereignty is what makes the U.S. Constitution so special.

Without a discussion of natural law as a check upon the power of positive law, and how natural law defines certain law concepts in republican constitutions, then American law schools teach nonrepublican law. In the absence of a discussion of natural law, then it is necessarily nonrepublican education. This is analogous to going to law school in Great Britain, where an artificial sovereign determines everyone's rights.

Lacking a basis in natural law and objective fact, American legal education today is based entirely on belief and opinion, which is religious education. A few false beliefs and opinions that go uncorrected in American education include: 1) that republican legislatures are the source of individuals' civil and criminal rights and duties, 2) that all U.S. citizens are positive law citizens, subject to Congress, 3) that judicial courts within the states have criminal jurisdiction over *malum prohibita,* which are regulatory violations under equity, 4) that positive law authorities can define facts of nature (such as case, crime, natural born Citizen, marriage and sex), and can define them subjectively, based on unnatural criteria, 5) that criminal statutes that are written only for the federal areas may be enforced within the states, 6) that all law serves the legislature, 7) that politically disfavored merchants are not owed administrative due process and equal protection, and 8) that natural law is irrelevant to the U.S. and state constitutions.

These false beliefs and opinions by attorneys manifests in American governments as a thorough muddling of all of the various jurisdictions discussed in this book, which instead are to be kept separate. This muddling of power results in – by definition – a *de facto* nonrepublican form of government, which serves only the positive law sovereign.

This is the result of people who either do not know or do not care about the rights of United States citizens to a republican form of government. Without a discussion and understanding of republics' judicial law jurisdiction – where adherence to natural law is a substantive right – then the republican form is not knowable, teachable or achievable.

The republican form of government has not been previously defined 1) because it has been forgotten over time, as will be discussed below, 2) because it has not been understood

162

so as to be taught, and 3) because there is no incentive for America's current power structure – which is nonrepublican in nature – to define the republican form or to teach it properly, which would emasculate this cabal's power.

To teach the republican form of government would preclude much of the wrongdoing of the U.S. and state governments today. It would preclude, for instance, the use of state judicial courts to enforce regulatory *malum prohibita*, such as traffic infractions, which are subject instead to administrative law courts. It would prevent adopted Citizens of the United States from running for or serving as U.S. President.

Such knowledge would also preclude the operation of the federal wars against unwanted drugs and guns, which are based on nonrepublican legislation that is applicable only in the federal areas. As we have learned, this nonrepublican regime is not to operate within the states, where the states and Congress may instead only regulate the commerce of property.

That criminal drug and gun prohibition is waged in Article III courts shows how far American governments have strayed from their federated republican model that was intended by the nation's founders. Because this model depends on the recognition of natural law, then to be blind to or to deny the role of natural law is to doom a republic to thoughtlessness.

The evolution of ignoring or forgetting the role of natural law in American republics likely goes back to the beginning of the United States. Americans have been mixed up about their governments ever since the U.S. Constitution was ratified.

For example, in the notes of Dr. James McHenry, one of Maryland's delegates to the Constitutional Convention in 1787, the author includes a famous anecdote about Benjamin Franklin on the convention's closing day.

"A lady asked Dr. Franklin, Well Doctor what have we got a republic or monarchy. A republic replied the Doctor if you can keep it," reads McHenry's entry.

In retrospect, Franklin could have been a little more accurate and candid. On one hand, he could have said "... a republic, if you don't forget what one is...," which essentially is what has happened. On the other hand, Franklin might have answered, "Both. You have gotten both a republic and a monarchy, if you can keep them separate."

If Franklin had merely uttered the latter response, instead of the one he supposedly said, then likely the entire national judicially-waged wars on drugs and guns would have been averted. This is because attorneys would have quickly realized that criminal prohibitions that Congress legislates as a nonrepublic for the federal areas are not applicable to drug and gun commerce within the republican states: 1) where crime is defined by nature as *malum in se*, and 2) where the U.S. and state governments instead regulate such commerce.

Perhaps Franklin did not know better. Perhaps few in his day realized that Congress legislates in two capacities, or that natural law defines such terms as case, crime and natural born Citizen, as readers of this book do now.

As we have seen, one cannot have a discussion about U.S. citizenship without discussing natural and positive law. This is because the nation has both natural law citizens and positive law citizens. Without knowing the role of natural law, then one has no basis to discuss the role and rights of U.S. citizens.

U.S. citizenship is based on natural science. All natural born Citizens have the DNA of their U.S. citizen fathers. Without having a basis in this natural scientific fact, one's view of republican citizenship is a mere belief or opinion.

This is analogous to discussing law's natural prohibitions called *malum in se* and equity's artificial prohibitions called *malum prohibita*. Without knowing their differences, without knowing the meaning of a crime in a republic, and without knowing the differences between regulation and prohibition, then republican criminal and administrative justice is simply not understandable or achievable.

This lack of knowledge has infected almost every single

American law-school graduate in the last one hundred years, including those on the U.S. Supreme Court. For example, that the Justices lack cognizance of natural law's role in citizenship law is evident in all major U.S. Supreme Court cases regarding citizenship.

For example, in *Minor v. Happersett* (1875), [169] which denied a female natural born Citizen the right to vote, no discussion was given to whether the equality of natural political rights applied to women or to voting. Natural political equality under natural law, as immortalized by the *Declaration of Independence*, was made no more relevant in the *Minor* decision than the weather in Washington, D.C. that year.

Thus, by 1875, most if not all Justices on the Supreme Court had forgotten, were overlooking, or were unaware of the natural law jurisdiction of the U.S. Constitution with regard to citizenship. This ignorance has contaminated most of the Court's decisions and omissions regarding citizenship rights.

Likewise in *Nguyen v. I.N.S.* (2001) the U.S. Supreme Court upheld Congress' disparate treatment of how unwed U.S. fathers and mothers secure their offsprings' political rights. They did this 1) without realizing that the provisions at 8 USC 1409(a) codify the natural law process of how U.S. males secure natural law citizenship for their offspring in the state of nature, and 2) without realizing that the provisions at 8 USC 1409(c) reflect how Congress bestows citizenship upon the offspring of U.S. females under its power of naturalization. The justices failed to mention the above important points because they were unaware of them.

Although the Court arguably reached a correct decision, i.e., that Nguyen's U.S. father did not properly legitimate his natural son to secure his U.S. citizenship, the logic of its argument was tortured. Both in the oral argument and the decision, the Justices groped for justification why Congress places greater requirements upon citizen fathers to establish U.S. citizenship for their children than it requires of mothers.

As we learned earlier, this is because there are no witnesses in nature to a man's role in creating offspring. This naturally requires the father to step forth and claim his children in order to secure their natural political rights in the political society. In the absence of a U.S. citizen father, then the mother looks to the positive law of her nation, or to the positive law of the place of birth, to secure political rights for her children.

Only knowledge of the meaning of natural born Citizen, and of the existence of the natural law jurisdiction in the U.S. Constitution, explains why Congress treats the offspring of U.S. citizen-mothers and citizen-fathers differently. [170] Thus, the discussion of any fundamental U.S. citizenship issue requires a discussion of natural law, which the U.S. Supreme Court has ignored or avoided in all its decisions on citizenship.

Consider as well that few if any of the justices on the Supreme Court seem to know the distinction between law and equity, and thus between criminal prohibition and regulation, which distinctions are fundamental to the maintenance of a republican form of government.

This ignorance of law and equity is apparent in *Gonzales v. Raich* (2005) where the Court upheld the authority of the D.E.A. to regulate a small California cannabis dealer. However, the Court cites statutory criminal authority, i.e., 21 USC 841 and 21 USC 844, for the D.E.A.'s regulatory actions, which criminal authority is applicable only within the federal areas, and not within California.

Thus, the Justices (and all participating attorneys in the case) demonstrate that they were completely unaware 1) that Congress legislates in two capacities, 2) that the issue in *Gonzales v. Raich* was about Congress' power to regulate cannabis commerce (and not about its power to criminally prohibit it), and 3) that such power to regulate comes from 21 USC 822 and not from the criminal provisions which Justice John Paul Stevens cited, which operate only in the federal areas.

As far as I can tell, every participant in the *Gonzales v.*

Raich (2005) case 1) was unaware of which police power, i.e., regulation or prohibition, that they were discussing, 2) was unaware of which judicial power, i.e., law or equity, in which they were operating, 3) was unaware that criminal statutes, i.e., 21 USC 841 and 844, were being used to uphold U.S. interstate regulation of cannabis commerce, and 4) was unaware that these cited statutes are to operate within the federal areas instead of within California.

Gonzales v. Raich (2005) is an example of a Supreme Court and a justice system that, despite their participants' best intentions, are incapable of upholding the republican form of government and American federalism, except by sheer luck.

So is the case of *Obergefell v. Hodges, Director of Ohio Department of Health* (2015) [171] where the Supreme Court ordered every state to license and recognize same-sex marriages. Both the *Obergefell* majority and its dissent: 1) failed to recognize that there are two kinds of marriages in republics, i.e., marriage under law and marriage under equity, 2) failed to realize that natural law defines marriage at (common) law and that a legislature's positive law can define equitable marriage to be anything it wishes, and 3) failed to realize that all licensed heterosexual marriages today are equitable, which privilege the 14th Amendment requires to be dispensed fairly and equally.

Because what is constitutional within the United States is republican, then no constitutional discussion of marriage or citizenship is complete without discussing the separation between natural and positive law. However, whether in marriage or citizenship cases, sadly the Court rarely acknowledges, discusses, or seems to comprehend the roles of positive and natural law in the U.S. Constitution.

Citizens United v. Federal Election Commission (2010) [172] is another well-known controversial case that demonstrates a breakdown in America's republican jurisprudence. It is in part based on *First National Bank of Boston v. Bellotti* (1978), [173] which holds that the free speech rights of the 1st Amendment apply to artificial persons, such as corporations.

In both cases, the majorities falsely equate the privileges of artificial persons in equity, which are granted by legislatures, with the rights of natural persons in the law jurisdiction, which come from nature, are unalienable, and are secured by the Bill of Rights. Both cases reflect a judiciary that is unwilling to keep the republican roles and powers of law and equity separate.

As we have seen, the Bill of Rights does not apply to artificial persons. Instead, it is intended to protect natural persons from the beliefs and opinions of artificial persons.

In contrast, artificial persons are ensured administrative due process and equal protection by the 14th Amendment. These persons have rules to protect them, but these are not the same rules that secure the natural rights of natural persons, such as the 1st Amendment.

Plain and simple, all artificial persons are subjects of positive law. As creations of legislatures, they have only the rights – including only the political rights – that these sovereigns grant them, if any. These rights may not be granted by the judicial branch. They do not exist outside of legislative positive law.

Artificial persons are not constitutionally entitled to free speech and the protections of the Bill of Rights, the latter which was established to secure individuals' natural rights. They are not entitled to any rights granted by judicial courts. Artificial persons are entitled only to the privileges and immunities that legislatures have granted them. The scope of these privileges are strictly political questions, subject to legislatures.

Thus, both *First National Bank of Boston v. Bellotti* (1978) [174] and *Citizens United* (2010) [175] represent fundamental carnage to republican law. These cases accorded rights to artificial persons in equity that belonged only to natural persons under law. Because law and equity are to be kept separate, then these holdings violated the Separation of Powers Doctrine.

This is to say that the political rights of artificial persons are solely political questions that are subject only to republican legislatures. This positive law authority does not legislate over the natural political rights of individuals. Judicial courts have no authority to make up such rights for artificial persons or to find them anywhere but in statutes.

Conversely, this is also to say that the republican form of government is not even remotely a political question, subject to definition by a legislature. In fact, the form exists solely because a national political sovereign, such as a king or legislature, is not in charge of defining it. A republic is a self-evident, constitutionally-secured, non-legislative, naturally predefined and inherent form which is to be recognized, understood and upheld by the judiciary – just like people's other natural rights.

Because individuals are naturally endowed by their Creator with certain unalienable natural rights, and because only republican governments have a judicial law jurisdiction that secures these rights, then logically, one has a natural right to a republican government merely to secure these rights.

Because the republican form of government is a natural right, then it belongs to all individuals everywhere. And being an inherent natural form, it always has.

However, outside of a conscious effort by people to discern the republican form of government and to institute a government based upon republican principles, then the concept of natural rights is meaningless. In a nonrepublic, where natural law is denied, then only the artificial rights granted by the political sovereign are recognized, which certainly exclude subjects' natural right to a republican form of government.

That the 1st Amendment does not apply to artificial persons, as the Supreme Court in *First National Bank of Boston v. Bellotti* (1978) [176] and *Citizens United* (2010) [177] contended, and that government can politically silence artificial persons, is inherent in republican governments' power to regulate. Because regulation includes the power to shut down businesses based on *malum prohibita*, then this is an effective, legal and inherent way for government to silence such artificial persons.

As we have seen, all that republics constitutionally owe to all artificial persons is administrative due process and equal protection. [178] America's republics can silence political speech of artificial persons by enforcing *malum prohibita*, if due process and equal protection are secured. In contrast, because legislatures have no authority over natural persons, then legislatures cannot silence the exercise of their 1st Amendment rights.

Let us take some extreme hypotheticals of *malum prohibita*. Suppose that the Occupational Safety and Health Administration (O.S.H.A.) holds the beliefs and opinions that newspaper ink is carcinogenic, or that televisions put out carcinogenic radiation.

O.S.H.A. owes these businesses only administrative due process and equal protection. Given this, for reasons of public health and safety, it enjoins all newspapers and all television broadcasters under its jurisdiction from doing business until these conditions are ame-liorated.

But this regulation or ruling would not violate the 1st Amendment, which does not apply to these corporations. Nor would it affect the rights of individual journalists, bloggers and citizens, whose 1st Amendment political rights operate in and are secured in a separate judicial jurisdiction, i.e., law, from that which rules corporations, i.e., equity.

The Bill of Rights secures, for example, the political rights of individual journalists from artificial positive law authorities, as well as the rights of natural persons from a government based upon opinion and belief. However, these amendments do not protect the creations of positive law, for example news, political or religious corporations, from the world of beliefs and opinions of their legislative creators.

The Bill of Rights does not and never was intended to secure the rights of artificial persons. These organizations are not entitled to a religious-free sovereign (1st Amendment), to a right to bear arms (2nd Amendment), to a right of due process of law (5th Amendment), to a right to a speedy criminal trial (6th

Amendment), to a right to a common law jury trial (7th Amendment) or to a right not to be cruelly punished (8th Amendment). Their political rights are strictly political questions that are defined by Congress and state legislatures, who could change or even end their corporate form of business at any time.

Artificial persons are subject to positive law. Individuals' 1st Amendment rights are not. The latter rights are above and opposed to the power of legislative positive law. They answer only to *malum in se*, such as shouting "fire" in a theater.

So, artificial persons do not have natural rights to speak, journal, contribute money and vote. Only natural persons in America's republics have these rights. For most Americans, these rights are naturally inherited – and are not bestowed.

Artificial persons are subjects of their creators and – if given administrative due process and equal protection – can be alienated by government from their privileges in a variety of ways and at any time. Their privileges are alterable and not unalienable because they are bestowed and artificial.

Thus, the above several cases, along with their critical flaws in jurisprudence and logic, demonstrate a fatal ignorance of the republican form of government that each of the Justices in these matters took oaths to support. The majority opinions also reflect an ignorance of jurisprudence as a science, which is to be based on objective and natural criteria.

Without recognition of nature's role in republican law and jurisprudence, of the separation of natural and artificial persons, and of the separate subject matter jurisdictions of law and equity, then the above failures in the republican form of government and in its jurisprudence were inevitable.

This is not to forget that the U.S. Supreme Court has overseen the judicially-waged war on drugs and guns throughout the United States for the past fifty years, which such wars can only be waged in Article I courts of the federal areas. Nor can we overlook that it allowed a 14th Amendment Citizen of the United States to unlawfully occupy the U.S. presidency, and to make two unlawful appointments to its bench.

There are, of course, exceptions to the Court's disregard of the republican form of government and federalism. For example, *U.S. v. Bond* (2014), [179] discussed earlier, accurately describes Congress' criminal power within the republican states. But this is an exception, not the norm.

To uphold the republican form of government is to recognize the duality of natural and positive law within the U.S. Constitution, and to understand the natural law basis of case, crime, property, marriage and natural born Citizenship, for example. This uniquely grounded and sane form of government embraces natural law to define the moral use of power.

For the U.S. Supreme Court to be ignorant of the self-evident natural law basis of the U.S. Constitution, and how natural law defines critical concepts that secure the republican form of government on behalf of its citizens' rights, exhibits educational and professional malpractice at their highest level. Particularly given the Court's public duties and intellectual resources, there is no excuse for its ignoring of nature's role in American law.

Non-arbitrary and just law

As we have seen, political morality – what is right and what is wrong in a polity – is defined by the Golden Rule. We have defined the physical violations of the Golden Rule, i.e., to harm someone's person or property rights, as naturally wrong.

Almost all societies agree that doing harm to others' person or property is a basis of civil and criminal court action. Injuring others is a near-universal moral and legal wrong. In a republic, doing others harm is the only basis for civil and criminal liability against individuals.

Republican courts are open to injury, and not to people whose person or property interests are not in some way harmed by others. In contrast, nonrepublican courts are open to anyone who offends the will of the sole political sovereign.

In a nonrepublic, if a political sovereign does not like certain behavior, then it can criminally prohibit it. The political sovereign's authority over its subjects and other subject matter has nothing to do with what is naturally right and wrong. The artificial nature of the sole political sovereign must deny the role of nature in establishing standards and its legitimacy.

In a republic, given the duality of natural and positive law, then a violation of another person's natural rights is the basis of the government's _only_ authority over individuals. Thus, what is naturally right and wrong has _everything_ to do with the political sovereign's authority over natural persons. Defining what is naturally right and wrong draws the line between the political sovereign's delegated authority and the reserved power of individuals who delegated it.

So, both social morality and civil justice in a republic – and the morality of civil justice – are based on enforcing physical violations of the Golden Rule – i.e., to do no harm to others. Trespassing other people's natural rights to their person or property, which is _malum in se_, is the exclusive subject matter of the law jurisdiction which dispenses natural justice. Legal, positive law rights (including most contractual rights) are adjudicated in non-criminal equity.

Because in a republic both political morality and justice are defined by the Golden Rule, which is a natural law or universal truth, and because in a nonrepublic morality and justice are defined by positive law, which is Man's law, then 1) only a republic approximates and maximizes natural justice by universally and naturally defining right and wrong, and 2) only a republic is free of the arbitrariness of Man's changing positive law. This is because Man's arbitrary law does not define a republic's unalterable law jurisdiction over natural persons.

Writing the above sentence caused me to recall a term I recently found in _Black's Law Dictionary_. The term is _law arbitrary_. Its definition reads: "Opposed to immutable, a law not founded in the nature of things, but imposed by the mere will of the legislature."

Other than republican constitutions, all of Man's positive legislative law is *law arbitrary*. It is law "imposed by the mere will of the legislature," it is opposite and "opposed to immutable," and it is "law not founded in the nature of things," meaning upon natural law. Thus, *law arbitrary* is the opposite of natural law, which is immutable, is non-arbitrary, and is not subject to a legislature. Natural law is not a politcal question.

Republics recognize that positive law will be unbridled *law arbitrary* unless it is bound down by natural law to make it non-arbitrary and just toward individuals. Thus the republican form of government is the only non-arbitrary and just form because it is based on natural law.

Under previous manifestations (or prototypes) of the republican form of government, such as in ancient Greece and Rome and in the southern United States, slavery was allowed. In other words, slavery was allowed by the supreme positive law of these areas, i.e., their constitutions.

This positive law which allowed slavery was *law arbitrary*. Slavery existed solely as a bestowed privilege from the positive law of human law makers. It was "not founded in the nature of things" – that all people are created equal.

In fact, slavery was in complete contradiction to the republican standards 1) of right and wrong, i.e., the Golden Rule, 2) of equality under the law, and 3) of the natural, objective and verifiable standard of justice owed to all natural persons.

Ultimately this means that slavery can only exist in a nonrepublic, and that the monarchical form of government of Great Britain, where a king granted some people positive law power to enslave others, lingered within the United States until slavery was constitutionally ended within the states by the Civil War and the 13th Amendment.

The ratification of the 13th Amendment was one of the great days in the history of the United States. It resulted from the realization that slavery is fundamentally incompatible with the republican form of government, and that natural political equality is worth fighting for.

From that point forward, all citizens could be enslaved 1) only by an American government, and not by other persons, and 2) within America's republics only for the commission of a crime, which we know is *malum in se*. Only when slavery ended, and all people were recognized as having the same natural rights to their liberty, did the United States adopt a republican justice system.

From that point forward, by design, the nonrepublican government lingered only in the federal areas, subject to Congress' plenary powers. From that point forward, the United States became a beacon of equality under law.

Then, with the ratification of the 14th Amendment, due process of law and equal protection became the law of the land for all persons within the states. This equality before the law operates outside of the proverbial law of the sea in the federal areas.

Now granted, the right to vote did not immediately get recognized in every citizen by the 14th Amendment, as it should have. Some non-whites and women were prevented from voting in the United States until the 15th and 19th Amendments were ratified.

This is to show that even the best examples of the republican form of government do not necessarily live up to the principle of political equality, as dictated by natural law. But eventually, and quite naturally, whether by war or by reason, these republican issues in America were properly resolved.

Likewise, republics can momentarily regress or be voided, as the republican form of government was under the administration of Barack Obama. As a 14th Amentdment citizen – born on U.S. soil to a foreign father – he had no natural political right 1) to be the chief political leader of the United States, or 2) to represent the natural political rights of natural born Citizens.

This makes Obama's occupancy of the White House lawless – outside of natural political law. Without a natural right to be President, he subverted the natural political authority of the office. In defiance of natural law, he became a *de facto* king.

As we discussed earlier, people who act like kings within republics are to be treated as criminals. By definition, they are predatory because they violate the natural political rights of others, and they do this with force, theft or fraud.

The occupation of the Oval Office by a Citizen of the United States violates the rights: 1) of all U.S. citizens to have a natural born Citizen President, 2) of all natural born Citizens to be the sole pool from which Presidents are chosen, and 3) of all U.S. citizen-fathers to be to sole source of U.S. Presidents.

Because judges and other attorneys have been unfamiliar with the meaning of a republican form of government, and its basis in natural law, then this and other *law arbitrary* has gone unchecked.

What would Jesus be? [180]

I started and I end this book in the same manner – with a reference to the law profess^or Jesus of Nazareth. Natural law's Golden Rule, which Jesus professed and which Hooker and Locke saw essential to society, is in fact the basis of the only moral form of government, which is the republican form.

This republican form is based on the duality of natural and positive law. Jesus' statement to "render unto Caesar the things that are Caesar's, and unto God the things that are God's" [181] indicates his understanding of this duality.

Jesus knew that a society which does not recognize natural law – and people's natural right not to be subject to other people and their positive law – cannot be just because it robs individuals of their consent authority. This was the nature of the temple tax that Jesus famously protested. Giving to the temple had been voluntary for the Jews before the Romans' occupation of Judea.

176

Thus Jesus knew the basis of a just society and of a just government. It was to separate the natural law from the positive law, to separate objective truth from religion, and to recognize both God and Man as dual sovereigns, thereby separating what is natural and compulsory from that which is artificial and voluntarily entered or consented to.

By his words and deeds, Jesus believed in separating the natural sovereign jurisdiction of individuals from the jurisdiction of positive law. This makes his political thinking republican, and opposed to the nonrepublican form of Roman government, which was based solely on obedience to positive law.

Jesus' christ-consciousness (and crime) was to worship God's law instead of Man's law, to know their differences, and to keep them separate. As a law professor, he espoused the principle of a separation of powers, starting with the separation of natural law from positive law. In general, American law professors today are unaware of this primary separation of power.

Jesus was republican 1) because he believed in natural law and natural duty, which only republican governments recognize, 2) because he recognized, understood and endorsed the duality of natural and positive law, upon which republican governments rest, and 3) because the republican form of government is the only self-evident moral form, for only it supports political equality and what is morally good.

Thus, the republican form of government is based on the teachings of the world's best known professor of natural law: Jesus of Nazareth. However, this does not render the republican form to be Christian or religious.

Although Jesus claimed that the Golden Rule "is the essence of all religion", [182] which could be a false translation, it is really the essence of all political morality, not just Christianity. For a government to uphold the Golden Rule as a law standard makes that government moral, but not necessarily Christian.

As we have seen, the republican form of government is uniquely moral 1) because it is based on the equality of natural

177

rights, and 2) because of its principle that positive law must be consented to. Both of these natural law principles are expressed in the *Declaration of Independence*.

As we have also seen, the republican form of government is uniquely rational and sane 1) because it is not based on false and unprovable supernatural claims of power (backed by fraud and force), and 2) because its justice is based on natural and objective criteria, instead of subjective belief and opinion.

Given that the Golden Rule is the basis of America's moral and sane republican form of government, the principle should be exalted. Given that it is not a religious rule, but is instead the natural basis of secular government, Americans should be regularly reminded of this most basic and natural political duty.

The reasons that America's republics have not reminded citizens of the importance of the Golden Rule is 1) because its role in the republican form of government has been forgotten and thus not taught, 2) because it is falsely understood to espouse religion, which the 1st Amendment says is to be kept separate from government, and 3) because to discern it and to teach it might logically, naturally and eventually end the non-republican form of government, with its inherent inequalities, which falsely operates throughout the fifty United States today.

The republican form of government is where the Golden Rule – a natural political law – is enforced as the nation's law standard. It is where natural political equality is upheld.

America's republican form is where the laws of Man are subordinate to the political laws of nature. If understood and practiced, this form naturally and exclusively precludes one man's rule over another.

As with the terms case, crime, marriage and natural born Citizen, America's republican form of government has inherent meaning and is a fact of nature, defined by natural law. When such form gets separated from its natural law basis, and its law jurisdiction, then it ceases to be republican.

178

Index

184

186

18th Amendment: 117, 119, 132
19th Amendment: 5, 98-102
21st Amendment: 117, 119

U.S. statutes

5 USC 3328: 97
8 USC 1101(22): 93-94
8 USC 1101(38): 93-94
8 USC 1304: 56-57, 152-153
8 USC 1401: 56-57
8 USC 1409: 53-57, 76, 94, 97
Title 18 USC: 134, 148-149
18 USC 7: 74, 132, 135, 141, 150
18 USC 922: 147-148
18 USC 923: 147-148
Title 21 USC: 149
21 USC 802(15): 78
21 USC 802(22): 78
21 USC 802(27): 78, 92
21 USC 822: 78, 92, 147-148
21 USC 841: 146-147, 166-167
21 USC 844: 166-167
21 USC 882: 83
26 USC 7203: 147-149
50 USC 3802(a): 95

Indiana Constitution

Article I, Section 1 (1816): 14, 67
Article I, Section 1 (1851): 14
Article I, Section 37 (1851): 34, 118 fn 94
Article II: 71

Article VIII (1816): 118

Indiana statutes

IC 4-21.5-3 *et seq.*: 91 fn 83
IC 34-24-1-3: 112 fn 92
IC 34-28-2-1: 80 fn 80
IC 34-29-2-1.5: 80 fn 80
IC 35-48-1-18: 78
IC 35-48-1-26: 78
IC 35-48-1-27: 78, 92
IC 35-48-3-3: 67, 78, 92, 92 fn 85, 112 fn 92

Case law

Andrews v. Russell, 7 Blackf 474, 477 (1845): 15 fn 20
Arizona v. United States, 567 U.S. ___ (2012): 128
Austin Lakes Joint Venture v. Avon Utilities, Inc., 648 N.E.2d 641 (Ind. 1995): 92 fn 84
Beebe v. State of Indiana, 6 Ind. 501 (1855): 14-15, 33-34, 39, 40
Bevans v. United States, 16 U.S. 336 (1818): 73
Bond v. United States, 134 S. Ct. 2077 (2014): 135-136, 172
Caha v. United States, 152 U.S. 211 (1894): 133-134
Citizens United v. Federal Election Commission, 558 U.S.

1 Author Kurt St. Angelo is an alumnus of the University of Lund, 1977 (Sweden); Pomona College, 1978 (Claremont, CA); the Robert H. McKinney School of Law – Indiana University, 1986 (Indianapolis, IN) and Toastmasters International. During the past thirty years, Kurt has practiced appellate law, been an entrepreneur, been active in the Libertarian Party, and written or co-written a dozen screenplays.

2 *The Pledge of Allegiance* was composed by Colonel George Balch in 1887. It was revised by Francis Bellamy in 1892 and formally adopted by Congress as the pledge in 1942. The official name *The Pledge of Allegiance* was adopted in 1945. The last change in language came on Flag Day 1954 when the words "under God" were added. Source: Wikipedia

3 Republican form of government, *A Law Dictionary* by John Bouvier, Revised 6th Edition, 1856, Constitution Society http://www.constitution.org/bouv/bouvier.htm

4 *Minor v. Happersett*, 88 U.S. 162, 176 (1875)

5 Republican form of government, *A Law Dictionary* by John Bouvier, Revised 6th Edition, 1856, Constitution Society http://www.constitution.org/bouv/bouvier.htm

6 *U.S. v. Wong Kim Ark*, 169 U.S. 649, 18 S.Ct. 456, 42 L.Ed. 890 (1898). "Citizenship by naturalization can only be acquired by naturalization under the authority and in the forms of law. But citizenship by birth is established by the mere fact of birth under the circumstances defined in the constitution." (¶ 113 at https://www.law.cornell.edu/supremecourt/text/169/649)

7 Kurt St. Angelo, *BUSTED – A Whistleblower's Guide to the War on Drugs* (Amazon Kindle, 2015) https://www.amazon.com/BUSTED-Whistleblowers-Guide-Americas-Republics/dp/069248678X/

8 *Yick Wo v. Hopkins*, 118 U.S. 356, 370 (1886)

9 Sovereign, *Black's Law Dictionary*, 5th *Edition*, p. 1252

10 Plenary, *Black's Law Dictionary*, 5th *Edition*, p. 1038

11 Paul A. Guthrie, *Demonic Positivism and the Science of 'natural born Citizen"* (Amazon Kindle, 2015), pp. 30-37 https://www.amazon.com/Demonic-Positivism-Science-natural-Citizen/dp/1511911816/

12 Artificial person, *Black's Law Dictionary*, 5th *Edition*, p. 104

13 Sir William Blackstone, *Commentaries on the Laws of England* (1752) ed. George Sharswood (Philadelphia: J.B. Lippincott, 1893), Volume 1, Book 1, p. 40

14 Paul A. Guthrie, *Demonic Positivism and the Science of 'natural born Citizen"* (Amazon Kindle, 2015), pp. 30-37 https://www.amazon.com/Demonic-Positivism-Science-natural-Citizen/dp/1511911816/
15 Thomas Jefferson, *Rights of British America* (1774)
16 John Locke, *Second Treatise on Civil Government* (1690), Chapter II, Of the State of nature, Section 4
17 *id.*
18 Article I, Section 1, Indiana Constitution (1851)
19 Article I, Section 1, Indiana Constitution (1816)
20 *Beebe v. State of Indiana,* 6 Ind 501, 508-509 (1855) citing *Andrews v. Russell* 7 Blackf 474, 477 (1845)
21 Science, Google definition
22 *The Bible:* Matthew 22:15-22, Mark 12:13-17, Luke 20:20-26
23 John Locke, *Second Treatise on Civil Government* (1690), Chapter II, Of the State of nature, Section 4 [b]
24 John Locke, *Second Treatise on Civil Government* (1690), Chapter II, Of the State of nature, Section 7
25 Richard Hooker, ed. John Keble, *Laws of Ecclesiastical Polity* (1594) Book 1, Chapter viii, 7. http://anglicanhistory.org/hooker/1/
26 *The Bible,* Matthew 5: 43 – 48
27 *Lex spectat natura ordinem,* says a legal maxim. *The law regards the order of nature.*
28 Sir William Blackstone, *Commentaries on the Laws of England* (1752) ed. George Sharswood (Philadelphia: J.B. Lippincott, 1893), Volume 1, Book 1, p. 40
29 Article I, Section 12, Indiana Constitution (1851),
30 Sir William Blackstone, *Commentaries on the Laws of England* (1752) ed. George Sharswood (Philadelphia: J.B. Lippincott, 1893), Volume 2, Book IV, p. 5
31 *State ex rel. Johnson v. White Circuit Court,* 77 N.E.2d 298, 300-301 (Ind. 1948)
32 *id.*
33 *id.*
34 21 Am Jur 2d Criminal Law § 1 (2008)
35 John Locke, *Second Treatise on Civil Government* (1690), Chapter II, Of the State of nature, Section 5, quoting Richard Hooker, ed. John Keble, *Laws of Ecclesiastical Polity* (1594) Book 1, Sec. 7 http://anglicanhistory.org/hooker/1/

36 Sir William Blackstone, *Commentaries on the Laws of England* (1752) ed. George Sharswood (Philadelphia: J.B. Lippincott, 1893), Volume 1, Book 1, p. 40

37 Sir William Blackstone, *Commentaries on the Laws of England* (1752) ed. George Sharswood (Philadelphia: J.B. Lippincott, 1893), Volume 1, Book 1, p. 40

38 John Locke, *Second Treatise on Civil Government* (1690), Chapter II, Of the State of nature, Section 5, quoting Richard Hooker, ed. John Keble, *Laws of Ecclesiastical Polity* (1594) Book 1 http://anglicanhistory.org/hooker/1/

39 John Locke, *Second Treatise on Civil Government* (1690), Chapter II, Of the State of nature, Section 7

40 No one thanks government for a good bowell movement. One thanks God or nature.

41 In re Duncan, 139 U.S. 449 (____)

42 John Locke, *Second Treatise on Civil Government* (1690), Chapter II, Of the State of nature, Section 4

43 natural rights, *Black's Law Dictionary*, 5th Edition, p. 925

44 For a more thorough listing and discussion of natural rights, see my book *BUSTED – A Whistleblower's Guide to the War on Drugs* (Amazon Kindle, 2015) https://www.amazon.com/BUSTED-Whistleblowers-Guide-Americas-Republics/dp/069248678X/

45 *Beebe v. State of Indiana*, 6 Ind 501, 510 (1855)

46 *Beebe v. State of Indiana*, 6 Ind 501, 508-509 citing *Andrews v. Russell* 7 Blackf 474, 477 (1845)

47 *Beebe v. State of Indiana*, 6 Ind 501, 510 (1855)

48 See also Indiana Code 1-1-2-1

49 *Beebe v. State of Indiana*, 6 Ind 501, 510 (1855)

50 Thomas Jefferson, Letter to M. D'Ivernois, 1795.

51 *Yick Wo v. Hopkins*, 118 U.S. 356, 370 (1886)

52 This echoes John Locke's statement about liberty, i.e., that it is about ordering one's own affairs "without asking leave, or depending upon the will of any other man." John Locke, *Second Treatise on Civil Government* (1690), Chapter II, Of the State of nature, Section 4.

53 *Yick Wo v. Hopkins*, 118 U.S. 356, 370 (1886)

54 Emmerich de Vattel, *The Law of Nations, or The Principles of the Law of Nature Applied to Nations and Sovereigns*, Book 1, Chapter IXX, Section 215, HTML version, Constitution Society http://www.constitution.org/vattel/vattel.htm

55 Paul A. Guthrie, *Demonic Positivism and the Science of 'natural born Citizen"* (Amazon Kindle, 2015), p. 133
https://www.amazon.com/Demonic-Positivism-Science-natural-Citizen/dp/1511911816/
56 https://www.uscis.gov/policymanual/HTML/PolicyManual-Volume12-PartH-Chapter2.html#S-B
57 Paul A. Guthrie, *Demonic Positivism and the Science of 'natural born Citizen"* (Amazon Kindle, 2015), p. 150
https://www.amazon.com/Demonic-Positivism-Science-natural-Citizen/dp/1511911816/
58 See Article I, Sections 2 and 3, U.S. Constitution
59 Emerich de Vattel, *The Law of Nations, or The Principles of the Law of Nature Applied to Nations and Sovereigns*, Book 1, Chapter IXX, Section 214, HTML version, Constitution Society
http://www.constitution.org/vattel/vattel.htm
60 naturalization, *A Law Dictionary* by John Bouvier, Revised 6th Edition, 1856, Constitution Society
http://www.constitution.org/bouv/bouvier.htm
61 naturalized citizen, *A Law Dictionary* by John Bouvier, Revised 6th Edition, 1856, Constitution Society
http://www.constitution.org/bouv/bouvier.htm
62 See 8 U.S.C. §§1401, 1408 and 1409
63 Deoxyribonucleic acid
64 *Steinkauler's Case*, 15 Op.Atty.Gen. 15 (circa 1875)
65 *Perkins v. Elg*, 307 U.S. 325 (1939)
66 Citizen of the United States, *A Law Dictionary* by John Bouvier, Revised 6th Edition, 1856, Constitution Society
http://www.constitution.org/bouv/bouvier.htm
67 Males' rights, powers and loyalties attach only to territory. Their biological role is to stake out territory and to secure inhabitants' rights within these territories. They secure these rights from invasion or usurpation by other male societies. All rights that males naturally secure for their offspring attach to this territory. They cannot bestow or secure citizenship rights from societies created by other males.

In contrast, as discussed in the body of this book, females' ties to society are not territorial. They can naturally go from society to society and create natural law citizens by the males of those societies. Therefore females look to males to establish natural citizenship for their children. And therefore, females have exclusive power to decide both the nationality and type of citizenship of their children by their choice of father(s) for their children.

As well, the positive law authority from a female's nation may choose to award naturalized citizenship to her offspring based on her nationality or based upon the positive law authority of the child's place of birth.

68 *Nguyen v. Immigration and naturalization Service*, 533 U.S. 53 (2001)

69 *id.*

70 Because of this, as my previous book on the war on drugs shows, there is no constitutional, statutory or case-law authority for America's drug war. It operates completely outside of and impervious to positive law, not to mention the natural laws of logic and liberty.

71 *Hilton v. Guyot*, 159 U.S. 113,163 (1895)

72 Religion, *Black's Law Dictionary*, 5th Edition, p. 1161

73 Belief, *Black's Law Dictionary*, 5th Edition, p. 141

74 *Yick Wo v. Hopkins*, 118 U.S. 356 (1886)

75 *Beebe v. State of Indiana*, 6 Ind 501, 519 (1855)

76 *Summers v. Earth Island Institute*, 555 U.S. 488, 497 (2009)

77 *Citizens United v. Federal Election Commission*, 558 U.S. 310 (2010)

78 Article II, Indiana Constitution (1851)

79 *Bevans v. United States*, 16 U.S. 336 (1818), Lexus Nexus headnote on page 3 of 22

80 See *Bevans v. United States*, 16 U.S. 336 (1818)

81 See *U.S. v. Wong Kim Ark*, 169 U.S. 649, 18 S.Ct. 456, 42 L.Ed. 890 (1898). Here the U.S. Supreme Court differentiated naturalized Citizens of the United States from natural born Citizens, writing: "Citizenship by naturalization can only be acquired by naturalization under the authority and in the forms of law. But citizenship by birth is established by the mere fact of birth under the circumstances defined in the constitution," i.e., that natural born Citizens are naturally produced by U.S. citizens and naturally inherit their parents' rights.

82 8 USC 1401 and 8 USC 1409

83 John Locke, *Second Treatise on Civil Government* (1690), Chapter II, Of the State of nature, Section 7

84 A caveat to the above paragraphs is that real property in America is not allodial. Allodial means "free; not holden of any lord or superior; owned without obligation of vassalage or realty; the opposite of feudal." Instead, real property in America is owned with obligations

to a superior. As we shall see, these duties operate in the equity jurisdiction, whose sovereign is the legislature. Thus, at least it can be argued that legislatures can declare cannabis growing on <u>their</u> land as *malum prohibita*. However, this would at most mean that the state would only have equitable power to shut down and enjoin such personal production, not the power to criminalize it.

85 In Indiana, this judicial power is codified at 34-28-2-1 and 34-29-2-1.5

86 Equity, *Black's Law Dictionary, 5ᵗʰ Edition*, p. 484

87 Sir William Blackstone, *Commentaries on the Laws of England* (1752) ed. George Sharswood (Philadelphia: J.B. Lippincott, 1893), Volume 1, Book 1, p. 40
http://oll.libertyfund.org/titles/blackstone-commentaries-on-the-laws-of-england-in-four-books-vol-1

88 See Indiana's Administrative Order and Procedures Act at IC 4-21.5-3 *et seq.*

89 *Austin Lakes Joint Venture v. Avon Utilities, Inc.*, 648 N.E.2d 641, 645 (Ind. 1995)

90 IC 35-48-3-3(i)

91 *Melvaine v. Coxe's Lessee*, 6 U.S. 280, 325 (1804)

92 *Minor v. Happersett*, 88 U.S. 162 (1875)

93 Kurt St. Angelo, *BUSTED – A Whistleblower's Guide to the War on Drugs* (Amazon Kindle, 2015) https://www.amazon.com/BUSTED-Whistleblowers-Guide-Americas-Republics/dp/069248678X/

94 *id.*

95 *id.* at 400 - 445

96 *Truax v. Corrigan*, 257 U.S. 312 (1921)

97 In Indiana, see IC 34-24-1-3(a)

98 In Indiana, see IC 35-48-3-3(i)

99 Thomas Jefferson: Reply to the Citizens of Wilmington, 1809. ME 16:336

100 *Ohio v. Helvering*, 292 US 360, 369 (1934)

101 Article VIII, Indiana Constitution (1816)

102 See Article I, Section 37 Indiana Constitution (1851)

103 *Gonzales v. Raich*, 545 U.S. 1 (2005)

104 Article I, Section 8, Clause 3 U.S. Constitution

105 Article I, Section 8, Clause 4 U.S. Constitution

106 Article VI, Paragraph 2 U.S. Constitution

107 See *Arizona v. United States*, 567 U.S. 387, 132 S.Ct. 2492 (2012)

108 *Gonzales v. Raich*, 545 U.S. 1 (2005)

109 *Wong Wing v. United States*, 263 U.S. 228 (1896)

110 28 USC 1251(b)(1)

111 See Article I, Section 8, Clauses 3 and 4, U.S. Constitution

112 8 Code of Federal Regulations Section 1003.1

113 *Extraterritorial Application of American Criminal Law* by Charles Doyle, Congressional Research Service, 7-5700, www.crs.gov, 94-166, February 15, 2012, page 1

114 Article I, Section 8, Clause 6, U.S. Constitution,

115 Article I, Section 8, Clause 10, U.S. Constitution

116 Article I, Section 8, Clause 10, U.S. Constitution

117 Article I, Section 8, Clause 10, U.S. Constitution

118 Article I, Section 8, Clause 15, U.S. Constitution

119 For example, agents from the U.S. Treasury Department - and not local police - investigate cases of U.S. currency counterfeiting.

120 See *License Cases*, 5 How. 504, 46 U.S. 600 (1847)

121 Grand jury indictment against Timothy McVeigh and Terry Nichols http://law2.umkc.edu/faculty/projects/ftrials/mcveigh/mcveighindictment.html

122 *Jurisdiction Over Federal Areas Within The States, Report of the Interdepartmental Committee for the Study of Jurisdiction Over Federal Areas Within the States*, April 1956, Part I and II

123 *id.*, April 1956, Part I, p. 13-14

124 *id.*, Part II, p. 105, citing *Bowen v. Johnston*, 306 U.S. 19 (1939); *United States v. Unzeuta*, 281 U.S. 138 (1930); *United States v. Watkins*, 22 F. 2d 437 (N.D. Cal., 1927)

125 *id.* Part I, p. 9

126 *id.* Part II, p. 106, citing *In re Ladd*, 74 Fed. 31, 40 (C.C.N.D. Neb., 1896)

127 *Caha v. United States*, 152 U.S. 211, 215 (1894)

128 Article I, Section 8, Clause 3 and 4 U.S. Constitution

129 *id.*

130 *Jurisdiction Over Federal Areas Within The States, Report of the Interdepartmental Committee for the Study of Jurisdiction Over Federal Areas Within the States*, April 1956, Part II, p. 107

131 *Cohens v. Virginia*, 19 U.S. 264, 429, 6 Wheat. 264 (1821)

132 *U.S. v. Fox*, 95 U.S. 670, 672 (1877)

133 *Bond v. United States*, 134 S. Ct. 2077, 2086, 189 L. Ed. 2d 1 (2014)

[2014 BL 151637]

134 Article III, Section 2, U.S. Constitution

135 *Palmore v. United States*, 411 U.S. 389, 412 (1973), Douglas dissenting

136 *Ostrow v. Samuel Brilliant Co.*, 66 F. Supp. 593, ___ (D.C. Mass. 1946)

137 *Hill v. Dorsey*, 22 F.2d 1003, 1004 (D.C. Cir. 1927)

138 *id.* citing *Keller v. Potomac Elec. Co.*, 261 U.S. 428, 443 (1922)

139 *id.*

140 *Kendall v. United States*, 37 U.S. 524, 526 (1838)

141 *Palmore v. United States*, 411 U.S. 389, 412 (1973), Douglas dissent citing *District of Columbia v. Thompson*, 346 U.S. 100, 104-110 (____)

142 *Hooven & Allison Co. v. Evatt*, 324 U.S. 652, 674 (1945)

143 *id.*

144 *id.*

145 Article III, Section 2, U.S. Constitution

146 5th and 14th Amendments, U.S. Constitution

147 14th Amendment, U.S. Constitution

148 *Palmore v. United States*, 411 U.S. 389, 397-398 (1973), citing *Gibbons v. District of Columbia*, 116 U.S. 404, 408 (1886)

149 *id.*

150 *id.* at 393 quoting *Palmore v. United States*, 290 A.2d 573, 576-577 (1972)

151 Article III, Section 2, U.S. Constitution

152 *id.* at 407

153 Article III, Section 2, U.S. Constitution

154 Article I, Section 8, Clause 17, U.S. Constitution

155 21 USC 822(a)(1)

156 Within the state republics, Congress may not license crime 1) because it has very little criminal authority there, and 2) because the political laws of nature and not Congress defines crime.

157 Admiralty law, *Black's Law Dictionary*, 5th Edition, p. 44

158 Maritime, *Black's Law Dictionary*, 5th Edition, p. 873

159 Maritime law, *Black's Law Dictionary*, 5th Edition, p. 873

160 *id.*

161 *Hooven & Allison Co. v. Evatt*, 324 U.S. 652 (1945)

162 Law of the land, *Black's Law Dictionary*, 5th Edition, p. 798

163 Plenary, *Black's Law Dictionary*, 5th Edition, p. 1038

164 *id.*

165 Kurt St. Angelo, *BUSTED – A Whistleblower's Guide to the War on Drugs* (Amazon Kindle, 2015) https://www.amazon.com/BUSTED-Whistleblowers-Guide-Americas-Republics/dp/069248678X/

166 *Ignorantia facti excusat, ignorantia juris no excusat.* Ignorance of facts excuses; ignorance of law does not excuse.

167 https://www.law.cornell.edu/anncon/html/art4frag16_user.-html#art4_hd68

168 Republican form of government, *A Law Dictionary* by John Bouvier, Revised 6th Edition, 1856, Constitution Society http://www.constitution.org/bouv/bouvier.htm

169 *Minor v. Happersett,* 88 U.S. 162 (1875)

170 This is another example of how the writers of constitutional amendments and statutes know the republican form of government – and thus law – better than most attorneys who work in or preside over judicial courts.

171 *Obergefell v. Hodges, Director of Ohio Department of Health,* 576 U.S. ___ (2015)

172 *Citizens United v. Federal Election Commission,* 558 U.S. 310 (2010)

173 *First National Bank of Boston v. Bellotti,* 425 U.S. 765 (1978)

174 *id.*

175 *Citizens United v. Federal Election Commission,* 558 U.S. 310 (2010)

176 *First National Bank of Boston v. Bellotti,* 425 U.S. 765 (1978)

177 *Citizens United v. Federal Election Commission,* 558 U.S. 310 (2010)

178 See 14th Amendment, U.S. Constitution

179 *Bond v. United States,* 134 S. Ct. 2077, 189 L. Ed. 2d 1 (2014)

180 Subtitled: "Jesus and his lawyers are coming back." Lyric from *Novocaine for the Soul,* The Eels

181 *The Bible,* Matthew 22:15-22, Mark 12:13-17, Luke 20:20-26

182 *The Bible,* Matthew 7:12